C000299139

Little Legs

Muscleman of Soho

By the same author

Homeless – But for St Mungo's

Little Legs

Muscleman of Soho

George Tremlett

UNWIN

HYMAN

LONDON SYDNEY WELLINGTON

First published in Great Britain by the Trade Division of
Unwin Hyman Limited, 1989.

UNWIN HYMAN LIMITED
15–17 Broadwick Street
London W1V 1FP

Allen & Unwin Australia Pty Ltd
8 Napier Street, North Sydney, NSW 2060, Australia

Allen & Unwin New Zealand Pty Ltd with the Port Nicholson Press
60 Cambridge Terrace, Wellington, New Zealand

British Library Cataloguing in Publication Data

Tremlett, George
Little legs: muscleman of Soho.
1. London. Persons of restricted growth.
Smith, Roy
I. Title
362.4′092′4
ISBN 0–04–440342–9

Set in 11 on 13 point Century Schoolbook by
Nene Phototypesetters Ltd, Northampton
and printed in Great Britain by
Billing & Sons Ltd, London and Worcester

Be not too hard for life is short
And nothing is given to man

September Song
by Christopher Logue

Preface

This book deserves an explanation.

I happened to meet Royston James Smith while researching my book about the men who live on the streets of central London.[1] Rather than describe their lives in the third person, I thought it would be more effective to interview a cross-section of them personally and tape record our conversations, trying to capture their speech patterns and means of self-expression. From my own work in this field I knew that the homeless had often been misrepresented, and that this blanket word covered a wide variety of people who had become homeless through illness, disability or sheer bad luck, or through having chosen to reject the values that most of us live by. My book was largely concerned with the pioneering work of the St Mungo Community Housing Association, and it was through their staff that I met Roy, which is the name we use in conversation, though he has many others.

When he was working in variety, his name was Little Jimmy or Jimmy Kaye, which is the one that appears on his Equity card. As a midget wrestler, he called himself 'Fuzzyball Kaye from the USA'. As a criminal in the London underworld, he was known as Little Legs, Little Roy or The Kernel, which was a joke around the Soho clubs because Ronnie Kray was known as The Colonel.

These names and his background emerged in our first conversations, in March 1988. It was then that I learned of his gypsy family and that he had been born deaf and dumb, only learning powers of speech and hearing after an accident with his mother's sewing machine at the age of 7.

Roy told me of his marriages and his children; his terms

[1] *Homeless – But for St Mungo's*, Unwin Hyman, 1989.

of imprisonment for crimes ranging from theft and deception to stabbing and manslaughter; his appearances in films with The Beatles, Elizabeth Taylor and Burt Lancaster; his meetings with Richard Burton, Marlon Brando, the Queen and Prince Philip; his seasons in pantomime at the London Palladium and in ice shows at the Wembley Empire Pool; his tours of the United States, Europe and the Far East as a circus performer and as a midget wrestler, and his years spent busking, spivving, street trading and running Soho clubs.

As we talked I realised that I had seen him before at other times in my life – when my father had taken me to the Festival of Britain, where Roy staged a midgets' side-show; at the Aston Hippodrome, when we all went to see *Babes in the Wood*; at various variety theatres in the days when my father was presenting shows of his own and Roy was working with The Three Monarchs, the Morton Fraser Harmonica Gang and Stan Stennett; and then later on the streets of Soho when I used to work for the *New Musical Express* at their offices in Denmark Street, and he would appear in doorways, suited and booted in those days, always wearing a natty hat, even when he was poncing or working as a strip club doorman. It would be hard not to remember him for Roy is only 4ft 2in. tall and there have never been that many dwarfs working in variety, or, for that matter, drumming up trade on the streets of Soho.

Nevertheless, I wanted to be sure of his story, and after he had told me of various newspaper reports about himself in *The Sunday People* and *The Daily Mirror* I searched through the microfiches in the British Museum Newspaper Library, and found them. When he told me of his wartime evacuation to Somerset and of the kindness shown to him by Lady Constance Ryder and Lady Audrey Anson, I searched through pre-war editions of *Burke's Landed Gentry* and *Debrett*, and found that his recollections regarding these two ladies were correct in every detail. I checked many of the dates he gave me with back numbers of *The Stage* and with *The Times Index* in Westminster Reference Library, and they tallied, although it has not been possible to check the dates of his criminal convictions and terms of imprisonment because many of these went unreported, and the Criminal Records Office at Scotland Yard would not supply details. The more checking I did, the more I realised that Roy Smith had a strangely moving story to tell that throws an unusual light upon many of the famous events and criminal trials of the last forty years.

One example of this was the Bissett murder case. This gave me great trouble because I did not know his name and neither did Roy. All he remembered was that a distant cousin had been sentenced to death, and that he had been on the the gypsy camp site when the murder happened and had quickly made himself scarce. That was forty years ago. I spent hours going through *The Times Index*. Each time I came up with a case that sounded right he denied it until, at last, I found the details of the murder of William Bissett, and confronted Roy with this in a coffee bar late one evening, just after he had finished busking the cinema queues in Leicester Square. 'Ssssssh. Keep your voice down,' he said, looking from right to left (and I am softly spoken). 'That was Slough, wasn't it?' It was, and there in the newspaper reports of the time was the statement that other gypsies had vanished from the site. Clearly, he had been one of them. I put some facts to him, without disclosing all my information. He filled in the remaining detail.

Being born a dwarf to a gypsy family who stored its caravans in a yard near to home in West Ham, Roy has always seen himself as a social outcast, although it has to be said that this has been largely through his own choosing. Other members of his family have lived wholly respectable lives. Coming from a Romany family with mixed Jewish blood, like the Krays, aware that many of his European relatives had been slaughtered in the Nazi pogroms, Roy has gone through life distrusting lawyers, police, politicians, or persons in authority. His parents taught him unusual skills to help him survive. His mother taught him sign language, which he still uses instinctively when distressed. His father got down on his hands and knees, teaching him to fight with fists and knives, and to live by his wits, which he has done, whether poaching for salmon and pheasants, catching rabbits with ferrets, totting, spivving, running for bookies, working in circus or pantomime, poncing or collecting protection money for the Krays.

When he spoke of his experiences with the Krays, I checked the names and the dates. They fit. Likewise, when told of many famous crimes, I cross-examined him carefully, slipping in trick questions, giving him surnames without Christian names to check his recall. Time after time he came back with missing detail that could only have been provided by someone who was there. As his story unfolded I realised that this revealed more about the Krays as people, and their lifestyle, than we have learned from other books about them, and that their 'firm' must have been similar in its internal, family relationships to those of many Mafia families as described by Pino Arlacchi in his definitive study, *Mafia Business*[2]. There were other moments when he carefully avoided giving me the answers I was seeking, always apologising, and explaining that he had no wish to incriminate himself or others.

As our conversations progressed over a period of several months, I began to realise that Roy Smith possesses a rare courage and an unusual breadth of knowledge, understanding that his willingness to talk *now* was due partly to his awareness of approaching death. His liver

[2] *Mafia Business* by Pino Arlacchi, first published in Italy in 1983, and then in Britain in a translation by Martin Ryle by Verso (1986) and Oxford University Press paperback (1988).

and kidneys often give him pain. His joints are weak and his sight is failing. He has been an alcoholic for many years, drinking two bottles of whisky a day, but seldom showing signs of drunkenness. He starts drinking as soon as he awakes each morning, but only takes a small sip at a time, drinking the whisky neat. As he eats very little food, this constant intake of whisky plays havoc with his internal organs. Most mornings he coughs up bile and has the shakes until he has had his first few sips.

His knowledge of the law is impressive, although it is one defined by a need to avoid its consequences. Likewise, he knows precisely how to avoid leaving forensic evidence when engaged in crimes of theft or violence. Many of his actions have been vicious, but only within tightly drawn parameters, for there is another side to him that is gentle and tender. This we observed at close quarters when he spent a week with my family as we neared the end of our work on this book; my children had chicken pox and he kept them amused with songs and jokes, conjuring tricks with cards, and tunes on his harmonica. Roy loves children, and possesses that real compassion for those less fortunate than himself which only the really disadvantaged understand, putting all his spare cash into raising money for guide dogs for the blind. (Remember: this is a homeless man with no money of his own.)

Had I wanted him to, Roy Smith would have told me this story for whisky-money. It was I who had to insist that there should be a proper legal agreement between us so that he should share fully in whatever success this book achieves. Since he was destitute when we met, I would have felt uncomfortable writing this book on any other basis. Should he die before the money comes in, as he sometimes thinks he might, his share will go to his daughter Karen, who was also born a dwarf, and who has been left to bring up her daughter, Georgina, single-handed since the death of her husband earlier this year.

In writing this book I used the same technique employed for my book *Caitlin*, which was written with the widow of the poet Dylan Thomas, using a tape recorder to capture the subtle inflections of speech and language that convey our thoughts; researching the subject matter with care; underlying the narrative with a firm structure, and then brushing across the surface again and again to check details of dialogue and description. There may be some mistakes, because Roy Smith is a man with a criminal past who instinctively destroys evidence and tells untruths unwittingly, but I have sought to avoid them. This is my book, but his life, and I have taken care not to allow my own opinions to intrude upon the narrative. The language employed is his. It is remarkably rich for although he is in no sense an educated man, Roy Smith uses a wide vocabulary, can vamp his way through several languages, is widely travelled, has a rare perception, and is essentially a proud man who believes that he has had a wonderful life, and would not have lived it any other way.

GEORGE TREMLETT
Laugharne
December 1988

Chapter 1

All my family were the same. Gypsies. Didn't give a fuck for no one. Now me, I'm a loner. People worry about me 'cos I'm a loner, and I carry all my money around with me in a cloth bag, but yer can't trust banks, can yer? People worry in case I'm mugged, but that doesn't worry me, 'cos they've got to bend down first to get me and by the time they do that I've got 'em by the neck, haven't I? Muggers don't stand a chance. Some have tried it. Two blacks tried to mug me one night, but I could see what was coming and like a silly sod I had the bag in me hand, but it still didn't get 'em very far.

I've had a lot of aggravation to put up with because of my size. Look at me knuckles. I'm only 4ft 2in., and my knuckles have all been broken, but no one has ever scarred me face. I'd kill anyone who tried to do that.

Gotta survive, duck and dive; that's the main thing. That's what my parents taught me.

We lived down Wallace Buildings, West Ham, opposite the Jewish cemetery, with our caravan and trailer parked out in the yard. Sometimes we were there, and other times out on the road, travelling, but that was where I was born. Number 50 Wallace Road. The biggest baby my mother ever had. She was a strong woman. When my sister Iris's husband died, she was the one who told her to pull herself together, but she would never, ever slap family. Neighbours, yes – but never family, although she would give my father one if he came home pissed. We were always having trouble with the neighbours. We had more money than they did and they didn't like it. We used to call them 'kippers and curtains'. That means they had net curtains up, kippers on the table, but nothing else in the house, although they still thought they were better than us because we were rough and ready and they were rather snotty. I used to slag them off.

My Mum's name was Helen, and her family was Jewish, which means I'm Jewish as well. She was born in what is now Israel, but they were Romany gypsies, real travellers, and they had relatives throughout central Europe. Lots of them died in the Nazi concentration camps, and before the war they changed their name from Marks to Paisley because Yiddisher people were having a hard time. My grandfather chose the name Paisley because he was in the rag trade, making ties and curtains, always using Paisley material. He lived to be 82, and died in 1940, working to the end. The other thing he done was shoe-mending. He had a big last or, as we call them, a hobbling-foot, and I used to help him. When he cut the leather, he tacked it first around the foot, then cut the leather off and pinned it right before nailing it down; then we used a rasp to file it all over, before polishing it with a heelball, nice and steady, around the edges.

My father's name was Harry, though some people called him 'H'. He had come down from Aberdeen, looking for work. He wasn't a big man but he was game and he could knuckle. He couldn't have been more than 5ft 6in., but if he gave someone a left hook they wouldn't know what day it was. My Mum would still knock him about, with a right-hander straight across the face, when he came home pissed. I used to stay up of a night with my Mum, worrying about what would happen when he came home, because she was his Guvnor. She hardly ever drank herself, just a drop of advocaat on our birthdays or at Christmas, but the old man was like me, a piss-artist. He would drink and drink and drink, but he knew the score. Once he came in that door, she would never leave him without a meal and he loved his stews and his fish-head soups, and on a Thursday she would cook him skate eyeballs, which was his favourite meal. Skate are dirty fish with a very big head. She used to take the top off, cut away the eyes, and that's skate eyeballs. That's where all the meat is. And then in the mornings, before he went out, Mum would make him a pot of strong tea, pour it into his pint mug with that Carnation sterilised milk, and then add one or two raw eggs, without breaking the yolks. He could never eat a breakfast, but that would give his stomach a lining.

The old man was a little tearaway and in the old days, before Reggie and Ronnie Kray came along, he was into everything. My Dad was number one around here [Soho], and down the East End. He was into street bookmaking [which was illegal in those days], totting, going on the knocker, spivving, scrap metal and all the con-games. Wherever there's shit, there's money. That's what he used to say. He was what we call on the cobbles, ready for a fight, and he'd done the sort of things with his life that I've done with mine. He had been a naughty boy, a street-fighter, but he'd only done remand. He hadn't done bird like I've done bird. When the Old Bill came round to get him, he would say, 'Right, then – take me!' He would put his knuckles up, and back up the front steps. He was game. There would be a bit of a punch-up, and then they would take him away in the Black Maria, which was what they had in those days.

With me being born deaf and dumb and a dwarf, he used to get down on his hands and knees to play with me. He used to toss pennies and I would watch him. Although my Harry boy was the eldest brother, I was the pet and we'd go down on the cobbles where he'd get two of the old large pennies, and then he'd flick them up in the air, or toss them, and while they were in the air you had to have a bet, Heads and Tails, Even Heads or Even Tails. Now, he was a gambler, a great gambler, and he taught me how to use the double-headed penny and how to throw a tail. In them days we were only gambling with a shilling or a tosheroon, but a lot of money could still change hands, and he'd have a couple of kids standing by to shout 'Dixie boy, here comes a copper' as soon as the Old Bill appeared; then they'd be slipped a toffee-apple and away we'd go.

The East End was different in those days, just before the war. There weren't so many motor cars. The muffin men used to walk around the streets of West Ham with a tray of muffins on their head, ringing a handbell. 'Muffins, your muffins, muffins I've got', ting-a-ling-a-ling, similar to the ice cream vans that come round now playing music, but then it was the bells. How they did it, I don't know, but I've seen market boys with three crates of apples on their heads, and boys down Billingsgate carrying the fish the same way. At weekends a woman came round with a donkey cart, and I can see her now, holding the wrong end of the walking-stick so that she'd tap the donkey's bum with the crook-end, holding the reins in her other hand. She brought round cockles, mussels, whelks, shrimps and crayfish. In those days you could get a pint of cockles for a penny. And then there were two old boys called Peacey and Dippy, or that was what we called them, anyway, and they had sweet stalls in opposition to each other down at the back of Manor Road. They used to go round the buildings where all the old girls used to hang their washing up, waiting for the kids to come out of school. Then going up towards Upton Park you had your fruit stalls and your rag trade.

My Mum was a tearaway. She wouldn't let anyone touch her kids, whether they were in the right or the wrong. If they tried to, she would sort them out. Up on the top floor in this block where we lived in Wallace Buildings there was a Mrs Elson, a big, fat woman, who tried to hit me with her broom. My Mum took the broom off her and then pulled her down the stairs. I don't know what I'd done, but after she'd finished with Mrs Elson, my Mum turned to me and said, 'Get in there.' She never touched our heads and never slapped our faces. If we were naughty we used to get it on the bum.

Mum kept the family together. Although she was a strong woman, about two inches taller than my Dad, she was gentle and loved us all. She was a very clever woman and I think she got it all from Israel. I've been to Israel and sent my kids there to work on the kibbutz, and I'm pretty sure that's where she got it all. While the old man was out on the streets, she would be doing the washing in the bath-tub and then throwing the sheets and the pillow-cases over the grass, which is the best bleach you can ever get, and then when we were living at West Ham she would bring home a little extra money by cleaning down at the school in Monega Road. It was a big school with four floors. Mind you, she wasn't on her own. She had what we called the washer-women working with her. I used to go down there to see me Mum and time it right, when they were having a tea-break, so that I could cop the biscuits.

She must have had a terrible shock when she learned that I had been born with my deformities. Deaf and dumb and a dwarf to boot. She had seven of us altogether, four girls and three boys, and I was the fifth, after my brother Harry and my sisters Iris, Helen and Elsie. My brother Raymond and my sister Mary came after me, and the funny thing was that I was a bigger baby than any of them, weighing in at 10lb 6oz at birth. It wasn't until some time later that Mum realised that my limbs weren't growing and I wasn't responding to sounds or learning to talk because I had been born deaf and dumb, although I could still scream from the throat to let someone know that I wanted something, or to draw attention to myself, and I could cry. She told me that I always screamed when I wanted to be fed. We never had milk bottles. My mother always used her breasts.

Mum used to take me down to the London Hospital in

Whitechapel, trying to find out what was wrong with me, and I used to hate it because all these doctors and nurses would gather round me, hitting me with sticks; testing my reflexes, I suppose, but I didn't know that then, because I was very young. All I knew was that every time I had to go down to the hospital they would hit me with sticks. They could see that my knee-caps are in two parts, one here (pointing to one part of his knee-cap, which is double-jointed), and one here (just below the other), and they could see that I couldn't straighten my arms. My mother took me to lots of other hospitals as well, to see different specialists, and they would always lay me out on their beds, while all these student doctors gathered around, all tapping me on the knee-caps and talking in whispers, and the only thing I looked forward to was that afterwards they would always take me downstairs and give me vegetables. I've always loved freshly cooked vegetables. I don't eat much meat these days. I'm almost vegetarian. When my Mum was taking me round those hospitals I was deaf and dumb as well, so I couldn't talk to them or ask any questions. They didn't know why I was deaf and dumb, although Mum told me later that she had been told that something might have frightened me, and then when I was 7 years old my hearing suddenly came and I was able to learn to talk, after all.

My Mum had one of those old-fashioned sewing machines with the pedals, and I must have been a naughty boy because I ran and slipped and fell over, cutting my head so badly that it bled. My mother picked me up bleeding, and she had me in her arms when she took me round to our neighbour, Mrs Hicks, the one neighbour with whom we used to get on very well. Mum put me on the sideboard while Mrs Hicks got some gauze or cotton wool and started to swab me where I was bleeding. I can remember my voice coming and my Mum started to stutter and cry. The first word I said was

'Mum', and she started crying, and said to Mrs Hicks, 'He, he, he, he, he ... he's talking'.[1]

With me still sitting there on the sideboard, Mum asked me to say the word 'Dad' and I did, and then she asked me to say 'love' and 'cry', and I can remember this all so clearly because she and Mrs Hicks were soon both crying themselves.

At that time, they still used to push me around in an invalid chair, although I could run around a bit at home. My legs were none too good and I couldn't walk far, because the weight of my body was too much for my joints. I am top heavy and sometimes my knees would go from under me. Later my Mum got me a pedal car so that I could move around and exercise my legs at the same time, and then she got me some roller skates. In those days you used to be able to go roller skating down the street, but you can't do that any more because the paving stones are none too clever. There was a girl called Doris Dawson who lived opposite and was a good roller skater. She used to take me down on the bus to the skating rink at Forest Gate, and it was she who taught me the toe-stop. And then later, when I was about 10 and we were out on the road, my parents got me a little pony called Molly, but I couldn't manage a saddle so I used to ride bareback. I'll never forget my Molly. They had to lift me up to get on her back, and then I never used the reins, just a halter, because my family, being gypsies, never believed in using a bit on a horse in case it cut her mouth. A halter was enough; you could just pull it gently this way (to the right) or that way (to the left), like steering the wheel of a car. I had her for about eight years and then sold her to a baker; they still had horse-drawn vans

[1] Every time he told me this story, Roy became distressed and started crying himself. There were moments when he became incoherent, unable to form words, and at such times he would instinctively start using sign language, which his mother taught him as a very small child. He told me that ever since this accident he has experienced an occasional loss of speech, usually when something has upset him emotionally.

in those days. That was the first time my Molly had ever worn a harness, so I got up on the trap with the baker and taught him how to lead her without having to use a bit. People shouldn't use bits on horses. It hurts their mouths.

Being little, I had a chip on my shoulder when I went to the Gainsborough Road School in West Ham. Because of my size I always had to sit at the front of the class, and with my legs being so short they didn't sit me on a chair because I used to get pins and needles (and still do) if my feet couldn't touch the floor. Instead, they would let me sit on my bum on the top of the desk, and later on someone made me a little foot-rest so that I could sit down at a desk like the other children. Kids are cruel, and I had to get used to them looking at me and saying things like 'Funny little man', 'Silly little dwarf', 'Short-arse' and 'Dwarf', and I would come home from school some days crying and sulking, saying to my Mum and Dad, 'Why can't I be as big as my brothers and sisters?' My Mum was very good. She was strict and she made me go to school, and my Dad started trying to help me stand up for myself.

My father had a heart of gold. He was a street bookmaker, but he would turn his hand to anything, like me. When you see a shilling, you gotta go out and get it, whatever you gotta do. He used to come out on the street down Leicester Square, down East Ham or Manor Park, wherever he had to go to make money, and was as game as they come. He may have been rough and ready, but he brought us all up well and I'm the only one who's ended up a villain.

When my sister Elsie was going out with a boy called Jim Bough, my Dad told him to join the police because although he was a tearaway my Dad always reckoned that that was the best side to be on. Elsie was working in the aliens department then at the Passport Office, and Jimmy went on to become Metropolitan Police champion boxer. He started off on a rough beat down at Plaistow. One night, four fellers chucked him in the river and he had to go to hospital, but Jimmy went on to become a chief inspector with the Murder Squad at Scotland Yard. Jimmy died of cancer, but he and Elsie had three sons and she's now living in Hillingdon where she's a councillor and a JP on the Uxbridge bench. Me, I'm neither Conservative nor Liberal nor bleeding Labour. I'm just me.

Elsie had a good voice, and at one time she could have made a career of it. She got a job singing with the Ted Heath Orchestra, but my mother was very, very strict and in those days show business, going on the stage, was disgusting, and although we were a gypsy family my Mum was dead against Elsie having a stage career. She had a wonderful voice, never needed a microphone, and I reckon she would have topped Vera Lynn if my Mum hadn't stepped in and stopped her going on with it. She spent six weeks with the Ted Heath Orchestra, and then my Mum took the cane out. That was when Elsie was 19. My Mum just said, 'You're staying here,' and when she spoke like that, we listened.

Elsie and Iris had a double wedding, not long after the war, and do you know what I bought them? A parachute. Material was short for wedding dresses in those days, so I bought them this material and we got a dressmaker to turn it into two dresses. Iris married a fellow called Geoff Huggett who had been in Australia. They ran a hotel near Southampton, and my sister Mary married Johnny O'Shaughnessy. They have a pub near Colchester. My brother Harry is married, too, and lives down at South Benfleet. The only one who's died was my younger brother Raymond who was a lovely, good-looking boy, trained to be an actor. He ran a club with me in Soho in the early sixties, and a protection gang came after him with hammers.

Being little, they all treated me like the family pet. Dad taught me all he knew to help me survive, because he knew that life was going to be hard for me. He used to get down on his hands and knees, teaching me to fight and handle a blade, and it's obvious that they were worried for me because of my size and because I was the only one who ever ended up before the courts. Mum and Dad came down to stand up for me every time. They had to, didn't they? I'm their blood. First time I was sent away to an approved school, Mum and Dad visited me once a month, but I had to prove myself. All the hard nuts had a go. 'Gimme a roll-up,' they'd say. 'Gimme this, gimme that.' And then I'd get what we call the wind-up, go to my peter, my cell – in those days you slept three to a cell – and they'd say, 'Why are you so small?', 'You should have grown, shouldn't you?' They would go on and on and on, and I would say nothing and then all of a sudden I would leap off me bunk and tell 'em, 'Now, cut it out! Shut your bleeding mouth. I'm laying down. I want to go by-byes.'

The happiest part of my childhood was being taught all the tricks of the con-game by my Dad, and being out on the road, travelling. He taught me everything he knew, and I'd sit up there at the front as he went round the streets or down in the country, working the knocker, totting, or doing the tweedle and the twirl.

When you go out on the knocker, you go from door to door, saying, 'I'm a traveller ... have you any gold or silver?' This is not totting; it's knocking. You always have to pay for whatever you pick up, and that way it's legal. Sometimes you let 'em see a roll of notes in your hand so that they can see you are ready to give 'em money, and that's when they start to show you their bits and pieces, and you tell 'em, 'Now all I'm paying for is the weight.' Then you take out the scales, which you always carry in your pocket, and weigh their gold and silver, paying so much per ounce. I've picked up a lot of gold that way. Rings, watches and waistcoat chains.

Totting is different because then you go out with the pony and cart, which was the way we did it, saying, 'Any old iron, any old iron?' and you pick up anything that's going, especially rags. The war killed the totting trade.

My old man used to do well at that game in the thirties, but then the government asked people to send in their iron railings and their pots and pans to be melted down to make aeroplanes, and you couldn't go totting after that. The government got it all. There was nothing left. You could still pick up the rags in the forties and the fifties, but that trade's been killed off too. It was all right when people had dustbins because you could always pick something up, but now that councils make 'em use those black plastic bags you can't see what's in 'em, and they smell. You can still go on the knocker, and some people leave bags of their own for rubbish, but it's not as good as it was. It was really naughty in the old days, because you'd be asking for old gold, silver, china and unwanted bits of furniture, and it was always elderly people selling their antiques. I've picked up half-hunters, watches, antique clocks, and once in Billericay I picked up a grandfather clock for five quid, and that was not so long ago; this geezer also had a double-barrelled shotgun, and I copped that too.

Rags are hard work, but you'd be surprised what they bring out, especially when they've had a death in the family. I've had brand new suits and overcoats, and some even better stuff in the pockets; gold watches and paper money. With the rags, you have to sort out the wool which can be unpicked and used in the rag trade (and there's always been good money in that), and then you chuck away the nylons and the cottons, which are crap.

My Dad also taught me the tweedle and the twirl, which is one of the oldest con-games of them all. That was one he used to do around the rag trade, or people running factories. Business people are always a little greedy, and they're the ones to go for. You go to them and say, always very polite, 'Excuse me, sir – someone recommended you to me. They said you might like to buy a nice piece of tom,' which is the word we use for jewellery.

'What you got?' they say, because they're always looking for something cheap, something they think has fallen off the back of a lorry, or whatever, and then you go into their office and show them your little white box, in which you may have a nice groin (a ring), a large diamond with a good cut. All the time you have another box in your pocket with a paste imitation.

'That looks nice,' they say, and this is what we call the tweedle, when they say, 'I must go to my jeweller and ask him to check it out'. You say, 'Of course, sir,' and you go along there with him if he wants you to, all the time keeping the other little box in your pocket, with the snide, the wrong 'un, tucked away inside. Often I say 'Yeah. I'll trust you,' and let 'em go off to see their jeweller on their own. I've done that many times. When they come back, they ask you how much you want – and I always say £700. I don't know why I do that, but it's like a lucky number.

'I'll give you a monkey,' they say, and that's the moment when you say, 'Sorry,' take back the little white box, and put it in your pocket, because you know that the greed is going to get them in the end, and they'll either go to their safe and get out the cash, or ask you to wait while they go down to the bank. While they're doing that, you switch the boxes – and that's what we call the twirl. It's one of the oldest tricks in the East End con-game, but it never fails because once they've had the tom valued by their own jeweller they never go back for a second opinion. They're happy and you're happy, and they take the groin home to the missus or the girlfriend, and she's happy, too. I've done that a million times, always for readies, and there's never any problem. These business people always like to feel they've got a sparkler on the cheap.

My old man was into all those tricks. He knew how to make the bees and the honey, but the best times were when we were out on the road, travelling around the fairs, or going from town to town, handing out the heather and the clothes-pegs, gathering around the fire in the evenings.

We never used to go to sleep Christmas Eve. It was a pillow-case job. When we were in the caravan we never knew which pillow-case was for us, and if we had been naughty and wouldn't go to bye-byes my Mum used to put a piece of coal in the pillow-case and then there'd be tears in the morning. We'd be crying and screaming, and then the other pillow-cases would appear with all the presents. 'That'll teach you,' she used to say. We never used to have turkey. It was always rabbits, pheasants or a grouse or a capon. We had a goose one year. That was good. We never roasted them; always boiled them in the pot with the vegetables, with the potatoes in a separate pot or cooked in their skins in the ashes, and then we'd sit around the fire in the evenings playing games, Ludo or Snakes and Ladders, and end up having a row over who was cheating whom. When you are out in the open, no matter whether it's cold, so long as you wrap up warm and you sit by a fire, you forget about the cold.

It was a peaceful life, really, because when you're travelling you think about where you are going, but you don't have to rely on anything or anyone because there's always plenty out there for you, plenty to eat, and plenty to do. You just go where you want and that's the freedom of it. You just trot down the road and do what you want to do. Once we pulled up in Bournemouth, and wanted some water. I knocked at this house with billycan in my hand, and they wanted to charge me two bob for it. I laughed at it, but paid them because we wanted to make a brew, and then later we got our own back. This house had a nice flower garden, with narcissi, so we took those; not for the flowers, but the straws. You suck them; they're good for you.

Another time, when we were staying at Hartlebury Common near Bromsgrove, my mother heard a noise and told me to come indoors. There was some fighting, and then Old Bill came and the ambulance,[2] and I realised from what I heard my Mum and Dad saying later that someone had died. That was a large camp, maybe sixteen or seventeen caravans, and when you're a kid you only pick up the bits and pieces, but that was the first time I had ever been close to violence. The two boys who got captured were distant relatives, and I mean *distant*, because when you're travelling you don't know who's your aunt and who's your uncle. You know who your brothers and sisters are, but you don't know who everyone else is. After they were sent away I never saw them again. All I can remember is that there was this 'accident' on the site, and that everybody said it was a bloody scene. As soon as the trouble started, Mum said, 'Indoors.'

We were shielded, really. Rough and ready, maybe, but still protected, and allowed to grow up in our own way.

[2]See Chronology, p. 200. A gypsy called John Loveridge died in the 'accident', and two of his cousins, William and Wisdom Smith, were gaoled for manslaughter.

Chapter 2

Our home at Wallace Road was right on top of the London docks, and we were bombed four times during the war. The first bomb fell shortly after the war started, and it wasn't long before us kids were evacuated. That first bomb wasn't a direct hit. It fell on the Jewish cemetery across the road. We should have been all right because we had an Anderson shelter at the bottom of our garden. After the air raid warning we all went down there, but my Mum came back to the house to make a cup of tea and the blast blew out all the windows and the kitchen sink clean out of the wall. The sink was made of stone and it fell across her legs, trapping her to the floor.

After that my Mum spent a long time in and out of hospital, because the weight of the sink and the force of the blast had broken her femur. They didn't have traction in those days so the doctors joined the pieces of her leg back together again with a steel pin.

Being so close to the docks there were air raid shelters all round the area so that people could take cover as soon as a warning went off. They even dug shelters across the road in the cemetery, down among the tombstones, and they became a favourite place to hide when we were kids. My Dad always wore a peaked cap and I used to nick one of those, believing that no one would know how old I was, and go down into the shelters with a packet of five Woodbines, also nicked off my Dad, and sit down there, Jack the Lad, having a quiet smoke. When they were digging the shelters, I'd say, 'Have you got a job for me?' and the men would never believe it because of my size, but I could always handle a pickaxe with one hand. The funny thing was that although I had been born with these short arms and legs, I always had plenty of muscle, and because the limbs had a shorter distance to lift or stretch, my muscles gave me greater strength than most people, which was to earn me a living years later.

With the bombs falling every night during the blitz, it was decided that all the children in the area should be evacuated. I cried, as it happens, because I had never been away from my parents before. My sisters Mary and Iris came with me, and so did my brothers Harry and Raymond. We were all told to report down at the Gainsborough Road School where the teachers gave us all a gas mask in a cardboard box, to sling across our shoulders, and a little bag of sandwiches and orange juice to keep us going on the journey. We caught a train from Paddington and then a bus met us at Taunton and we were taken to this massive mansion called Knowle, near Timberscombe, where Lady Constance Ryder and her sister Lady Audrey Anson looked after us like VIPs. We had never seen anything like it, and for us East End kids the next three or four years were the finest years of our lives.

Lady Constance and her sister were the daughters of the 4th Earl of Harrowby. Lady Constance had been born in 1871 and had never married. She was a JP for Somerset. Lady Audrey was four years younger, and in 1902 had married Major the Hon. Henry James Anson, of the 2nd Battalion, the Highland Light Infantry, who died two years later. Anson was a son of the 2nd Earl of Lichfield, and she had not remarried.

Eighteen of us were taken into their home which was the most luxurious place we had ever seen. Three drives led away from the mansion across the park, one leading to the road to Timberscombe, the second to Minehead, and the third to Wooden Courtenay. They also owned two farms and part of the river which used to get flooded. That was where I learned to love the trout; they came in swarms, similar to salmon, and you knew which way they were going so all you had to do was sit there, taking it easy, having a rest, and then you'd fish them out with a net. Nice fish; about a pound and a half. I used to go fishing for years after that, and years later, after we had gone back to London and I was about 16 or 17, I caught a large pike, using a worm on a rod and line – and he pulled me in.

Down at Knowle we had everything we could dream of. In the park they had ponies, and so I was able to ride bareback in the local gymkhanas. The sisters had separate herds of Jerseys and Guernseys, and they let me have a Jersey cow of my own as a pet. She was blind and we called her Bumbles. I used to take her around the fields on a halter. Now, a cow's tongue is rougher than a horse's and she used to lick me because she liked me, and that hurt; she always knew when I was there from my voice, and I was the one who was allowed to lead her into the milking shed and take her to her stool because they didn't have milking machines down there in those days. I used to sit down on the stool and milk her myself, straight into an enamel bucket. Jerseys and Guernseys don't give much milk, but it's the best; better than your Shorthorns, Longhorns, Friesians and Ayrshires.

Lady Constance was wonderful, a motherly sort of woman, really, although she had never had children of her own. She worried about me because I was little, and gave me a room of my own with a beautiful Chesterfield settee instead of a bed. There was an old battleaxe of a cook, Ma Chaplin, who cooked for us and for them, and she used to say, 'Royston, Royston – you're a naughty little elf!' because I was a right little sod all the time I was there, playing tricks, and going out across the fields, poaching rabbits, which I would leave on her kitchen shelf. They had three gamekeepers, but the main one was an old boy called Bolsie who had a 12-bore shotgun. He would never miss a bleeding rabbit, and used to take me out with him, shooting rooks through their nests. It's unfortunate, but rooks are pests and they've gotta go. I learned a hell of a lot in Somerset. I used to go picking whortleberries, which are like a blackcurrant, and it was good poaching country.

Bolsie taught me such a lot. He's well dead now but I can remember him well. He was a shotgun merchant and I said to him one day, 'Can I go out with yer?' He used to walk around the fields with his gun under his arm and a bag like a moneybag around his waist in which he kept two ferrets. He would stick them down a hole with no nets, and stand there waiting with his 12-bore. Then when the rabbits popped out, BANG! Then he says, 'I'll teach you how to do the snares,' and taught me to find their runs, the best places to put a snare, and how to set the pegs.

The rabbits were heavy for me because of my legs. One day, after I'd learnt a lot, I was out on my own, using fishing nets over the holes because I didn't have a gun. You could hear the rabbits coming. You sit on the ground and hear the pads of their feet as they run through the burrows, so you know when one is coming out. I heard this one running, and went to grab him in the net, but he came through so fast that he knocked me over on my back. Normally, you grab a rabbit by his back legs, put two fingers of your other hand behind his neck, and pull – quick. That kills them. But I have short arms and when I got this one in the net he started to fight me before I could grab his legs; then he clawed me to pieces, down my front, and got away – so I gave the ferret a slap!

Lady Constance ran the Wolf Cubs and the Boy Scouts, and Lady Audrey ran the Brownies and the Girl Guides, which we all joined along with the children from the village. Lady Audrey made us laugh because she used to fart a lot, and every time she did she gave a little cough to hide it. Anyway, they asked me to join the Cubs and kitted me out with a uniform, a green jumper and a beret with a scarf and a woggle, and they made me a sort of sergeant because I could recite the alphabet backwards, which nobody else could, and already knew deaf and dumb language, the Morse code and semaphore, which my Mum had taught me. My Mum was very clever, and had also taught me shorthand, not Gregg's or Pitman's, but gypsy shorthand, writing backwards and so then Lady Constance wanted me to teach all these things to the other Cubs and Scouts. I also showed them how to make a raft, and then I taught them tracking, which is another thing that gypsies are very good at, using sticks and stones to lay a trail.

One time I made a raft across the river with this other boy who was staying there, Harry Dale, who came from Bristol. Now, when you are a Boy Scout (or at least, in those days) you always had to have what they called a staff or a stave, and I used that to stick in the water and steer the raft across the river. Harry tried to cross the river without a stave, and got stuck halfway. I was on the bank and said, 'I'll give you a push' – and pushed him right in. He was always moaning, that Harry Dale. 'Everybody's always having a go at me,' he used to say, which was true, because we were kids, and that day I did. He fell right in. 'I can't swim,' he said, so I said 'Drown!' but we pulled him out in the end and you can guess who got the blame.

Another time while we were there one of the boys was killed. He had come from Lambeth and I can't remember his name, but he had been evacuated along with his mother and they were living behind the house in some flats above the stables. Knowle was a massive big place, with flats and cottages all around the house for the staff, the maintenance men, the herdsmen, the groom, the gamekeepers, the cook and the household staff, who all had accommodation of their own.

This boy got crushed when a dung lorry backed up against a wall. He was killed instantly, and all the Cubs, Boy Scouts, Brownies and Girl Guides went to the funeral with Lady Audrey and Lady Constance. This was in the Timberscombe parish church, and everyone was there for the service. His coffin was so little, and afterwards they carried him out to the graveyard and put him down the hole and we all walked past the open grave and gave him our salutes. I don't think most of them knew what to say, but my parents had taught me. 'Rest in Peace,' I said. Someone heard me and paid me a compliment, but who wants compliments?

Mum and Dad used to come and visit us, but they had to stay in Watchet and the two ladies used to send their chauffeur over there to pick them up, and I can remember walking up the drive to the house to meet my parents after not having seen them for a long time. We were all dressed up in our Cubs and Boy Scouts uniforms, and you can imagine what I looked like with my little legs wearing short trousers, my woggle and my scarf, with the badges down the jumper. My Mum couldn't get over it. She had to laugh when I went up to her and saluted her with my three fingers to my forehead, which is what we had to do, and then my Mum started tears again and crying, as I said, 'I want to come home, I want to come home.'

And then I did a very naughty thing. Lady Constance had let me have a pony and trap, which I used to take around the village collecting waste paper and cardboard that was sold to a scrap merchant to raise money for the Cubs and Scouts. One weekend I picked up a good load, sold it for £6 10s – and kept the money. Lady Constance called all the Cubs and the Scouts together on the lawn in front of the house, dressed me down in front of them like a court martial, and then snipped off all my badges with a pair of scissors, with me crying buckets and feeling so ashamed of myself.

It was my fault. I had been a naughty boy and had only myself to blame. It was humiliating but I wouldn't blame her for it. She was wonderful to me, really, and I think she loved me, in some sort of way, because years later, not so long ago, I was waiting to go into court at Bow Street for some minor little thing, causing an obstruction, and a woman comes up to me and says, 'Are you Royston?' and it was her niece who I'd known as a child. The family still remembered me, forty years later.

When I was taken ill down at Knowle, Lady Constance was very kind to me. She found me lying on the Chesterfield, doubled up in pain and called the district nurse, Nurse Leigh. 'He's in a bad way,' said Lady Constance, who then called Bolsie, who was her chauffeur as well as her gamekeeper, and drove her around in one of those big Austin limousines, and they laid me out on the back seat of the car and drove me into Minehead hospital where the doctors operated on me straight away. It was peritonitis. I got upset, because in those days they didn't give you a pre-med or a needle; they put a thing over your nose and mouth, like an ether or chloroform mask, and you went out for a little while. When I woke up I was back in bed, and I felt around myself and could feel these rubber tubes sticking out of my belly. There was a lovely looking little nurse on that ward, and as the weeks went by (because I was in hospital for nine months), I really fancied her. Although I was a youngster, my brain was working like a man's. One day she came in and asked me whether I would like some fruit, and I told her, 'You're nice. I fancy you.'

'You're too young to be saying things like that,' she says, and then she pops me into a bath and she can see that I really am fancying her.

'What do you know about sex?' she says, with me lying there in the bath, having this erection. 'You're too young for this!'

'Wanna bet?' I said, trying to convince myself that I stood a chance.

This was in either 1942 or 1943, long before the National Health Service started. It was private medicine in those days, and Lady Constance paid all the bills while I was in there, and came to see me regularly. She used to bring me in fruit juice and fresh apples and pears from her orchard, making quite a fuss of me. The war seemed very far away, and it never occurred to me that Mum and Dad might still be in danger in West Ham until one night, during a black-out, we looked through the hospital windows and saw British and German planes in aerial combat, having a dog-fight.

To cheer me up, my Dad brought my brothers down to see me in hospital, and they knew that the one thing I wanted, really wanted, above all else, when I came out, was a pony, so they bought me one. The pony, which I called Molly like another pony I've had, was waiting for me when I came out of hospital. I think they paid about five or six quid for her, and it was when I was riding her bareback that a hornet stung her bum and she threw me off. She went crazy, as horses do when they're stung, and I must have fallen badly because a big lump came out on the side of the belly where I'd had the tubes sticking out of me with the peritonitis. The lump was like a balloon, and that put me back in hospital for another nine months.

It all seemed so unfair, with me being little and having been deaf and dumb, and now finding myself back in hospital again for a second time. My mother was worried for me, as was my elder brother, Harry, who looked after me, even though I was a bit of a tearaway; I was their little pet.

That stay at Knowle came to an end soon after I came out of hospital. I went back there to live for a while, but Lady Constance and Lady Audrey were getting on in years, and it was getting to the point where we were really more than they could handle. Harry was allowed to go back home to West Ham because he was the eldest, but my brother Raymond and me were sent to live in a place called Crowcombe, which was also in Somerset, with me staying with this one couple and Raymond staying with the woman's elderly widowed mother next door. Raymond couldn't suffer it because she was always telling him what time he had to be home, and I wouldn't take no chat off the people I was staying with.

We were still going down to the village school at Timberscombe, but then I got into trouble again. The first time was when a boy called Billy Robinson kept calling me 'Dwarf' and taking the piss out of me. He said he wanted a fight, so I took him down by the river, pushed his head under the water, let him up, and then pushed his head back under. 'You shouldn't have done that,' he said. 'That's your bleeding fault,' I told him. 'You shouldn't take liberties.' I've had that sort of trouble all my life, but you can only take so much.

Then I got into even worse trouble inside the school itself when another boy was taking the piss out of me. I jumped up on top of the desk, grabbed the window cord, and tied it round his neck, twisting it like a garrotte. I must have been 12 then, and if the teacher, Mrs Willis, hadn't stopped me, I would have killed him. Around about the same time my mother had inherited a house at 301 Strone Road, Manor Park, East Ham from my Auntie Nell, which meant that Mum and Dad could move away from the docks and take us all back to London, although I was still sent back to Somerset a few months later to go to an approved school over that business with the boy and the window cord.

I had a few months with my parents before being taken back to Somerset to go to this approved school, which was at Blue Anchor, and during that time I got my first job in panto, playing Bonzo the dog in a Richmond Theatre production of *Babes in the Wood*. By then the doodle bugs were flying over the East End of London, and then came the V2 rockets.

We had an air raid shelter at Strone Road, a big one down the garden with wooden steps down into it, but we preferred to go down the coal cellar. We had this cat, Jimmy, that wore bells around his neck and went down the cellar with us. One night we heard the sirens go off to sound the All Clear, but my Mum said, 'We'd better stay down here a bit longer . . . I can hear another one coming over.' There we all were, sitting in the dark because we were in the black-out, waiting for this whirring engine sound to stop, because you knew that when that stopped the doodle bug would fall, but it wasn't a doodle bug at all. It was our Jimmy. I kicked him up the arse. Later we had the V2 rockets which we called the 'arse-alights' because they had flames coming out of their backsides. I saw quite a few of them but in East Ham we were safe, being those few miles further away from the London docks, which was what the Germans were after. Clever as always, my Dad got himself a good job. He went round the houses selling black-out curtains. He was shrewd, my Dad; never missed a penny and taught me a hell of a lot.

Dad was still into everything. He handled black market clothing coupons, tobacco coupons, sweet coupons and food coupons long after the war, instead of betting slips, when these old dears wanted a flutter. Then on Sundays he would dress up in his best suit, go down the pub, get himself a pint of bitter, and when he saw the old-age pensioners he would hand them back their coupons, saying, 'That's yours' and 'That's yours', all of them marked, because he knew which one was which. He was tough, but he had a heart of gold, and when I got sent away he and Mum tried everything to get me back home – and I was back within three months. They must have gone to the Appeal Court, but I was too young to know what had happened.

They tried to calm me down by giving me lots of pets. That's what a lot of parents do, isn't it? I had Dutch rabbits, bantams (which I bred), chickens and four ducks. I got one of those old-fashioned tin baths and dug out a hole at the back of Strone Road so that they could have their own pool, and then I would throw bread in. Ducks like to soak the bread in the water before they eat it. At that time we had Irish people next door, and one day this woman asks me if she could have two ducks for her children. Well, I gives her two and coming up Christmas-time I asks her, 'Where have the two babies gone?' And you know what they had done? Cooked them! Can you imagine what I done? Smashed all their windows. I knew it wasn't the kids. It was their Mum and Dad.

The first time I was in real trouble again was about a year after I got back home from Blue Anchor. My Mum was a bit short of bread, and I said to her, 'I'll be back.' She says, 'Where are you going, son?' and I told her, 'Just walking round the club.' There was a youth club just down the road with table tennis and all that, and as I goes down there I sees this car. I knew whose motor it was, and I didn't like the geezer. He used to sell shirts, a wholesaler, Jack the Lad. It was peeing down with rain and he had parked his car right outside his house. Now I can get into any car, so first I does his quarter-light, gets inside the car with me screwdriver, cuts the wires with me pliers (which I used to have with me wherever I went), and then takes his Motorola radio, which was a new thing in those days. They were expensive.

'Are you all right, son?' My Mum says when I come back home.

'I've just got to go upstairs a minute,' I tells her, but when I starts to fit the plug to the radio I realise that I've left part of it behind in the car. So back I go to get it, open up the bonnet, and as I'm down in there, with my feet up in the air, the Old Bill sees me. I nearly fell in the car, but I got away, though I stood no chance with my legs. All of a sudden, they are at the door.

'Have you got a little son?' they said to my mother.

'Yes,' she says, for she wouldn't lie. She would never do that, which is right, and the Old Bill put me in their car and take me down to the East Ham Town Hall police station.

'Do us a favour,' I says. 'Don't bang me up 'cos I gets claustrophobia...' So they sits me on their bench, and says, 'Now can we trust you to arrive in court tomorrow morning?'

'Yeah,' I says, and gets twelve months' probation.

Another night I'm going down the East End, down Stratford East, and this geezer says, 'Would you like to come home with me?' Now, if it had been a woman I would have been right there right away, but this was a bloke. In them days I didn't know what queers were, but he taught me. He said he had a house in Forest Gate and would give me some money. When we gets there I says, 'Excuse me, but can you give me a couple of bob now?' and he gives me two and a half quid, by which time I'm beginning to realise what he's after. There were three stone steps up from the street to his house, and I lets him go first and open the door, but he didn't get as far as the stairs. You can imagine what I did to him, as I told him, 'You dirty little sod . . . you want to make it with a dwarf.'

Chapter 3

Somerset has kept pulling me back. Over the years since the war, I have gone back there again and again, sometimes on my own, and occasionally with my parents, who were back to the gypsy travelling life once Peace had been declared. They liked Somerset, too. It sort of pulls me. I had a cottage there, for a time, and a lot of friends. It was a little thatched cottage.

The first time I went back was in that very cold winter of 1947. The snow lay thick on the ground for weeks, and you could tell where the lambs were trapped beneath it because the ewes would wait nearby, bleating, until the farmers came to dig them out. I went back to Timberscombe first, because I was getting a few quid, this way and that, doing naughty things, and could stay in the country pubs. From there I went on to Wooden Courtenay, Dunster, Orcombe and Minehead, where I went back to see the nurses who had looked after me when I had my operations. I liked the beach at Minehead. Then I went back to Taunton to see where my Mum and Dad had stayed at Watchet, and then on to Washford and Bridgwater. I spent sixteen or seventeen weeks travelling around because I had plenty of money.

Mum and Dad still had the caravans, and we used to take off every summer. No one ever knew when we were going or where. We just moved, and then when we came back we would leave the caravans down in Essex because we had nowhere to park them at Strone Road. My Mum didn't like going back to the house in winter, because if you are used to a van and a trailer you find it hard living in a house; it takes a long time to settle in.

That first summer we stopped at Ickenham first, and then covered all of Middlesex; then we went down to

Kent, before going on down to Somerset. Timberscombe had upset me because Lady Constance and Lady Audrey were dead and Knowle seemed delapidated after the war. The land and the farm seemed poorer. Behind the house they used to have an aviary with what I called Puss-in-Boots bantams, those black birds with the frills around their feet, and that had all gone and so had the breeding pheasants, the ponies and the shire horses. The stables seemed bare. They were quiet and empty, and the house didn't seem the same any more.

When we were travelling, Mum and Dad used to have the caravan and then the boys had one trailer and my sisters had the other. They were pulled by horses, not motors. We used to have eight horses, so that there were always two tied at the back, resting, while the others pulled the grais, which was our name for them. When we stopped, they all had to have their nosebag before we lit a fire and fed ourselves, although with us it wasn't a bag but a bowl of chaff and cows' cake. We always carried bales of hay and buckets of water, tied to the sides of the trailers. Once we had lit the fire, we never knew how long we would stay. Sometimes it would be just overnight; other times we might stay for months. We were always on the move, and I've still got a caravan on a piece of land that I own down in South Benfleet, which my brother Harry looks after for me, so that I can take to the road again one day if I want to.

Wherever we were camping, there was always a fire outside and my mother would have a big iron cooking pot hanging from an iron spit across the fire, all day long, which was why we called it hotpot. The pot was simmering all the time. There were always three pots, hanging side by side. One was this cooking pot; the other was for washing or bath water (because we always carried a tin bath with us wherever we went), and then there was a smaller pot which heated quickly, and that was for making tea, or whatever. We called the iron rod or spit, the pie; the cooking pot was the pikey, and the one with the washwater, the tub.

When you are travelling, your meal-times are your own. You don't have set times. If you've been out poaching, or whatever, and you come back a bit peckish, the stew is always there on the pie, and there's always water ready for a pot of tea. You don't need much money because there's always food to be had in the fields or the hedgerows; all you need is enough for your whisky and tobacco, because we used to poach most of the meat we ate and our vegetables we would pick up along the way. When you're travelling, there's always a field of swedes, carrots, potatoes, beans, or what have you, and the farmers don't miss the odd sackful. Our cooking pots, plates and cutlery would last for years, and apart from the baccy and the whisky the only other money you needed was for feed for the animals, although you'd often pick that up as well, as you went along; the dogs and the horses have to come first because they're the workers. Without them, you're stuck.

There were no motorways then and we would take as long as we liked to travel wherever we wanted to go. We were free. I only went to school when we camped near a village, but Mum was still strict. She taught me to read and to write, and so did my Dad, when he was sober. I never went to school regularly, but when we hit somewhere she would put us into school to get us out of the way for a couple of hours, but I couldn't suffer it. The longest time I ever went to school was at Timberscombe, where the lads made me a special desk in the carpentry lessons so that I could have support for my feet when I was sitting down. It was like a built-in foot stool.

When you are a Romany, everything comes to you.

We used to work the heather, but not like the women who work Oxford Street nowadays, with a little bit of silver paper wrapped around the heather. They're not real Romanies. They're what we call diddicoys or pikeys, not true travellers. When we used to do it, we always left the stalk on the bottom of the heather. You never charge for it. You just hand it out to people, going door to door or in a shopping street, and then you wish 'em 'Good Luck', and they give you whatever they want to give you. If you charge 'em, they don't give so much; but if you wish 'em 'Good Luck', they give you the money – and that's what we call 'a ding'. We used to pick the heather down in Somerset, on the Quantocks and around Dunkery Beacon, any time after the end of May, and then we would come back down to a little wood called Bow Tops, this side of Minehead, going towards Dunster. We would go down there every year, fill the caravans up with heather, and then work our way back up through the country till we got to London, giving the heather just the odd flick of water, because heather doesn't need too much water. Then we'd pick the whortleberries which make a very good jam; everyone wanted whortleberries in those days, and we also went round selling clothes pegs, which we used to make ourselves, cutting down the hazel twigs, trimming off the bark, cutting round the top to make the knob, slitting them up the middle with a knife to make the peg, and then boiling them over the fire in water before we rubbed them down with sandpaper. It was hard work but you could always sell them because there were no plastic pegs in those days.

Other times we would go out door to door, asking, 'Any old gold?' with the little pair of scales in our pockets, weighing the gold there and then on the doorstep, or we would say, 'Any old rags or lumber?' Sometimes I'd leave a printed letter on their doorsteps with a carrier bag so that they could leave stuff out for us, and then call back later. There's so much that you can do if you're a traveller.

I used to have a polecat called Michael. As good as gold, he was. A pet, although I took him out after rabbits as well. I used to take him on a lead. Polecats are so fast, and if you're not careful they'll shoot down the rabbit hole, catch a rabbit or the babies, open up their bellies and eat the guts. Then they curl up and go to sleep. When that happens, you have to get a shovel and dig the bleeders out. I had him for about two years. That's about their limit. Rats, mice, polecats; they don't last much longer than two years. Polecats change their coats in winter, like ferrets, and then when it gets cold, that's them finished. Once they've got a little belly on them they hibernate, similar to the grey squirrel which is like a rat. Once I was out poaching and all of a sudden I sees this burrow, a rabbit hole, and I could hear a little cry. I didn't have a walking stick with me, but a long cane with a hook on the end of it that I used for poaching pheasants. I poked that down the hole, and that was how I found my Sheila, the vixen, only a little cub. Puts her in the bag and takes her home to mother. God rest her soul, she says, 'What's that you've got there? It stinks,' because a fox cub can be near enough as bad as a skunk. I says to her, 'Let me do what I want to do with it. I'll keep her outside ... give me some bread and milk.' Mum would do anything for me, anything. She gives me the food every day, and I watch Sheila growing bigger and bigger. She just used to wait for whatever was left over, and never tried to get any of the food in the cupboard. I had her for a long time. She was better than any watchdog.

In them days I used to love a rabbit, and also went out catching moles. We would catch them and sell them for 6d each without cutting them, and then we learned that if we cut their bellies with a knife, like you do a rabbit, take out their guts, and then skin them and pin their skins to a board covered with saltpetre, we could sell them for double the money. A shilling a skin, in old money. We used to take them to the fur shops and sell twenty, thirty or forty skins at a time, but it was hard work because moles are tiny, much smaller than mink. I've sold rabbit skins, too, but I would never sell fox furs after rearing my Sheila.

I've seen women wearing the head and the tail of the fox around their collars, although you don't see so much of it now, and I don't like that. I don't approve of fox hunting and I don't like stag hunting, because it's spiteful and cruel, and not done for the right reasons. If I pop a rabbit, shoot it or snare it, then that's for food. I'm not hunting or chasing it. I'm killing it swiftly for food. If I put a ferret down a hole, the rabbit comes out – POP! It's all over. I don't hold with hunting because it prolongs the suffering and that's not necessary. Of course, being so little I could never carry too many rabbits at a time, but on a good day I would catch maybe three or four; cut their bellies and tip their guts out, and then take them back to the caravan, skin them, taking them by the back legs, and skinning them all the way down, over the head. Rabbit skins weren't much good. You could sell them sometimes, but not often.

I used to have these two cairn terriers, Foxy and Mincey, and I would take them out with me across the fields. One would go one side of a hedge and the other was trained to run down the other. You train them the same way you do a ferret; you give them a little bit. First of all, you give them bread and milk, and then you give them a bit of rabbit to give them the taste for it. That's cruel to be kind. Everything is cruel to be kind, but that gives them the taste, and once they've got it they'll hunt for you.

Dogs are best for poaching pheasants because you can have them working ahead of you, either side of the hedge, while you come on behind with the perch-pole, that's the cane with the hook on the end, like a fishing rod, and then you drop the hook or the loop over the pheasants' heads. They don't stand a chance because they're frightened of the dogs and they're such heavy birds that they have to have a run before they can lift themselves off the ground, like herons and the bigger seagulls. They just freak. Sometimes I would go out and find a pheasant on the nest, and then I'd just slide my hand under their bums, get their eggs and take them back home to rear myself. I'd put them under a bantam.

I've been poaching now for over forty years. The last time was only four years ago, down in Essex, and that was for pheasants. When you catch them, you have to pluck them well and they're hard. Then you cut their tongues and hang them up to bleed, like you do a hare, maybe two or three days, though you have to be careful that the flies don't get to them, especially in the summer-time. In winter, you can hang them for a week, but you still have to make sure there's no flies or bluebottles.

When you do a hare or a rabbit, you cut them down the belly and take the guts out, but with birds you pluck them and that's hard work, and the pheasant's the hardest of all. It's best to throw a bit of hot water over them first, and then always pluck them away from the lie of the feather, against the grain, so to speak, and then you've got to get the fluff off; there's always fluff left, underneath the feathers. Then there's the bit of quill left in the skin which you have to get off by holding them over the fire, burning it away and scraping them with a knife, and then you can do whatever you want – fry it, bake it, shove it in the pot. I prefer the pheasant in the stewpot, myself, cooked with all the vegetables, but not the potatoes. We always cooked the potatoes in a separate pot, or baked them in the ashes.

I like trout as well, especially when I can cook them myself, because I don't like any butter, margarine or oil; I just lay them in an oven and let them bake a little bit, and I also like sousing them in vinegar after they've been baked. Just leave them in the vinegar for ten or fifteen minutes with some pepper. We never throw away the heads. We pop them in a saucepan with a couple of eggs, a lemon and maybe a few vegetables, and then stew it. The same with salmon heads. They make a lovely soup as well, because they're a similar fish, like a cousin to the trout.

Once I got a goose and strung it up on the caravan door, bleeding it like I would a pheasant, and that was a bugger to pluck, but you still did it the same way, like you would chickens as well, starting at the tail, and pulling the feathers back against themselves.

Chickens and pheasants – I cook them all the same way because I'm a gypsy. I take the blade and cut their tongues, let them bleed, hang them for a couple of days, and then put my hand up their bums, and take their livers out. Sometimes a hen will have eggs without the shells inside them, and you take them out and fry them with the liver. Chopped liver. Beautiful, with a little bit of Mozzarella or paprika. Beautiful. It's a meal on its own. I don't like any of them roast or the fried stuff; boil them every time, because that's the way to get the flavour, always making sure that if you've got any cabbage in the pot, you separate off the green water with a mug, and eat that on its own with a little touch of pepper. Beautiful.

I've had hedgehog, too, but gypsies don't eat hedgehog as much these days as they used to. Years ago, they used to cook the hedgehog the old-fashioned way, wrapping it in clay and baking it, but I don't. I take a skewer and stick it right through its bum and out the other end, and then I cut its belly because they're full of worms and things like that, because that's what they eat. So you have to paunch it like you do a rabbit, take out all the guts, and then turn it over the fire, and when it's cooked you can take out the spikes, but you don't have to bother about too many of them because the only parts of the hedgehog that are really tasty are the legs and the breast. I've eaten snakes, too, out in Asia, where they keep them in an aquarium, let you choose the one you want, and then chop its head off in front of you, chop up the snake, and cook it over a little fire like a primus stove, until the juice runs out of the body like a soup.

If you're a gypsy you'll try anything because the food's out there waiting for you, in the fields and the hedgerows, and then you bring it back to the caravan. Then afterwards my Mum would have these lovely rice puddings, which she'd always have simmering away for hours on the open fire.

It was a wonderful life because every day was different, and out in the country the police used to leave us alone; I've never had any trouble with the police outside London, apart from once when we camped on a site near Slough. It was a large camp and there were a lot of people there, and some of the other guys brought back this bloke who they'd met down the pub. He was an old man and he'd been flashing his money round, and they rolled him, and later he drowned in the river. The Old Bill came along and picked up one of them, Joe Smith, who was probably a cousin, although I don't remember him; you're all one family when you're gypsies, and then we all made ourselves scarce. Joe was sentenced to death,[1] but then he was reprieved when they decided to stop topping people, and I heard years later that he had committed suicide.

That was the first time I had ever been close to a murder because when that other thing happened (the Loveridge case), my mother had told me to get back inside the van and so I saw nothing. This time we all made ourselves scarce, and later I got a message from the other guys who were there asking me to take care of a guy because they thought he had grassed us.

In the late forties, we still had the house in Strone Road and when we were back there I used to do a bit of dealing in ration books, tobacco coupons and clothing coupons, with a little bit of black market fruit and veg. Tomatoes and cucumbers, but not wet fruit. Eggs and chickens, too. I

[1] The dates are given in the Chronology, and Roy Smith's version does fit. Gypsy Joe Smith, as he was called, was reprieved after the House of Commons voted to suspend capital punishment in April 1948. This decision was reversed by the House of Lords. By then, Gypsy Joe was serving a gaol sentence instead. I have been unable to find any independent confirmation that he did commit suicide.

used to drive around the farms in Essex on my bike, and then when I'd done a deal with a farmer he'd bring the stuff up to the East End in his lorry. Those farms always had big kitchens, and I'd go in, sit down, and they'd say, 'Sssssh, I don't want to let Mum know', and then we'd get down to business and I would always get away with it because of my size. Sometimes I would even get a cow, a pig or a sheep because meat was rationed and they would always have the odd one or two hidden away on their farms so that the government inspectors wouldn't find them. I was a spiv. The smallest spiv in the East End of London, and I'd handle anything. I must have shifted tons, all around East Ham, West Ham, Manor Park, Ilford, Stratford, Woodford and Romford.

Between all this I was doing the odd bit of villainy, and every Christmas I would get a job in pantomime, usually playing the dog because of my size; every pantomime had to have a dog in those days, and I had to run down into the audience during the interval and let the children stuff my mouth with sweets and ice cream.

The first pantomime I did was at Richmond Theatre, and then the next year I was at Watford Palace, and I had a booking nearly every year after that; the only years I wasn't in panto was when I was banged up in Brixton or Wandsworth. That first year at Richmond, I used to travel over on the Tube every night. The fare then was 1s 6d and my wages were about £9 a week, so I was doing well, but I would still turn my hand to anything, like my Dad, and I'd always make the most of my size. By the end of September every year, I used to have a Guy outside West Ham station, collecting pennies for the Guy, and I used to pick up £2 or £3 a night because I suppose people felt sorry for me, not that I cared what they thought so long as I was making money.

I had to have the money because I had been on the drink since I was 13. When I was 15 I got myself a temporary job on a building site near Strone Road, and by then I was on the whisky. They made me the tea boy and gave me a little bike so that I could get around the roads and a large urn so that I could go to different parts of the site, shouting 'Tea up!' I'll tell you what happened next because it was so long ago that they'll never nick me for it now. There was this hut on the site, half of it was my little kitchen and the other half was the site office, and this man, Wally Newman, was the paymaster. He used to travel up every day from Southend. We didn't get paid until the Friday, but the money used to arrive on the Thursday and he would sit there in his hut counting out the wage packets, and I used to see all this money on his desk as I came in, saying, 'Mr Newman, would you like a cup of tea?' When he had done the wages he used to put them in his briefcase, and then popped them in the peter. He would lock the peter and put the key in his drawer, and it was all good money – plenty of silver, ten bob notes, pound notes, but no fives, which were difficult to handle in those days when there weren't so many about. Now I could lloyd the drawer, using a piece of plastic like a Barclaycard – a piece of lloyd (celluloid) – and you slip it through and the lock opens.

So I came in at night, just after seven, got the key, opened the peter and took the briefcase home. Then I borrowed my Mum's fruit dish and took it up to my room and started counting, having told her I didn't feel well. There was £750. All the nice music, the crispies, went under the mattress, but then I got scared the following morning because I thought my Mum, God rest her soul, being so clean and tidy, might turn over the mattress, so I told a good mate of mine, 'Look, I've had a little tickle . . .' Now, he wasn't a thief but I told him what I done, and said I was nervous in case my Mum found it, because then it would have been spanky bum-bums. So he looked after it, while I went back to work as though nothing had happened, and I was there when Wally Newman opened the safe, looked at it, and said, 'It's gone!' Then he shut it and opened it again, and then shut it again, saying again, 'It's gone!' because he couldn't believe his eyes, and I'm still standing there when the Old Bill came. Then while they're crawling all over the place, looking for fingerprints, I'm saying, 'Would you like a cup of tea, officer?' and I'm the only one they don't call in for questioning because I'm standing there, right next to them. I've always had good nerves; never had the shakes.

With that tickle I bought my Mum her first fur coat, a musquash dyed mink, but she never suspected anything because I went down the dog track at Upton Park and got a geezer there, a bookie, to give me a ticket saying I'd won the money on the dogs, weighing him in for a tenner. We went back home and my brother Harry told me Mum, 'What do you think this little sod has done? He's backed a winner!'

'Oh, you naughty boy,' she says. 'You're just like your father,' but she was right pleased when I took her up East Ham High Street and bought her the coat, and there was plenty left over; that job kept me going for a long time. Seven hundred and fifty quid was a lot of money in those days; two years' wages for most people.

Before long I could open any peter, and I've done hundreds since, but never been captured. The only things the Old Bill have ever captured me for are blags and deception.

Over Stratford, a mate of mine who is brown bread now, God rest his soul, gave me a message that there was this geezer down Stratford Broadway who used to come out of the bank, regular every week, with a big briefcase. 'OK,' I says. 'Let's have a look.' So we clocked the geezer and we could see that he was carrying money, and so I says to my mate, 'Are you gonna take it or is it mine?' He says he doesn't fancy it. Now Stratford Broadway had cobblestones then, and I waited until the geezer came out of the bank, then gave him a push, copped the bag, and got in the motor. And what do you think he had in there? Twenty-five quid and a fucking great Savoy cabbage!

I was getting known down the East End, and other lads were wanting to work with me. I had John McVicar trying to work with me once, when he was 17 and as skinny as a rake. I was going out on a job and I had the Butlers with me then; two half-caste boys, good lads, Jimmy and Ray Butler, who used to graft with me. We went off, did the business, and then came back to the Black Lion pub where Soppyballs, McVicar, says to me, 'Did you have it off?' Now, you never talk business in a pub because you never know who's listening. So I gave him a right talking to. Told him to shut his fucking mouth. Anyway, his mother had a tobacconist's and confectionery shop down in Burgess Road, East Ham, just by where the Palace Theatre used to be, and the next day he comes to me and asks me to rob his mother's shop. Now, I'm thinking that his mother might want the insurance money, and that's OK, but he says, 'No, she won't know anything about it!' I wouldn't have nothing to do with the geezer after that. A bloke who would rob his own mother! He's a preacher now, a reformed character, who writes books and goes on the telly, but I would never trust him after that. Would you rob your mother? Would I rob my mother? Who wants to rob his own mother? And then he gets captured, and becomes a big strong man in the nick, weight-lifting and all that caper, but it doesn't matter how much muscle you've got when you're at it; you've gotta have the bottle as well. I wouldn't let him work with me. No chance. I still says he's a wanker.

When I first started getting into trouble with the police, my Mum didn't handle it too well, but the old man wasn't so worried. He thought I was a great little feller. 'There's no one like you, son,' he used to say, and I think he was proud of me, because although I was the smallest I was making my own way, and never had no chips on my shoulder. I would turn my hand to anything, just like him.

Now, there was a lot of money in metal. There always is, especially in bronze, copper and even lead. Back in those days, there were so many of those Victorian lead roofs and there was good money in them. Lead is fucking heavy, but what we used to do was climb up on the roof with a Stanley knife, cut through it in slices (because lead cuts easy), and then roll it up and drop the rolls over the edge of the roof. That's another good thing about lead; it doesn't make any noise. When you drop a roll from a roof, it doesn't ring out like bronze or iron. There's just a dull thud, and then you slip it into bags, which is the easiest way of carrying it, with one of you at each end.

In the days I'm talking about, you could get £26 a hundredweight for lead, which was good money, because money was worth a lot more then than it is now. I'd go anywhere for a good load of lead. I did this one job in Bury St Edmunds, but when we got there we found that the railway store, which was what we had been sent to, was packed with copper tubes and copper fittings. I'd better not mention the name of the mate I went down with, but there were two of us and we propped a railway sleeper against a wall and got in through a window. There was all the copper, and piles of boxes. I opened up one really big carton and inside it was packed with chamois leathers, great big ones, as big as me. 'That'll do me, fuck the copper,' I thought. We only got £50 for the copper, but there were 400 chamois leathers in those cartons and we sold 'em to a fence for £1 a piece.

In between all these jobs, travelling with the family, working in panto, and so on, I would have a go at anything. When the chance came to go to the United States to work in a circus, I jumped at it because I was game, and I think that's why I started making friends with the Krays.

When I was about 18, my two brothers got called up to

do their National Service in the army. They both went into the Airborne Artillery, the Red Berets, and that really gave me an inferiority complex for a time. I would have loved to have done something like that. My Mum phoned the recruiting office and said, 'I've got another son. He's 4ft 2in., and he would like to do his part . . .' No chance, but the military people still came to arrest me some time later, when I was appearing in panto in Birmingham, because I hadn't filled in the call-up papers. Now, there was a chip then; I could do the business, bless 'em, better than my brothers, and this was when I started getting really naughty. All I wanted to do was devilment. To get some spunk out of me.

So I goes down to Stratford and into the Black Bull where I meets this mate of mine Bill [name deleted] and his mate [name deleted]. Now, they always used to say to me, 'Are you game?' and I say, 'What for?' and this time they tells me about a three-hundredweight peter down at a garage. Now I've got my Thames van, and I always worked alone, and although I'm little, with my small arms my biceps are extra powerful, so I take the van down to the garage, back it up to the door and load on the peter. It took me ages, but I did it. Then I found I couldn't get the front open, so I took off the back with the hacksaw, cold chisel and a hammer, and that took me bleeding hours – but I copped another 750 quid, and was well in the money again.

By this time I had got to know Reggie and Ronnie Kray. After working the halls in variety, I had met up with a girl singer, Heddy Horden, and we were living in a small flat, not much bigger than a bedsitter, in St Stephen's Gardens, Paddington. Realising that I had got something with my muscles, I had taken up weight-lifting and body training and used to drive over to the East End every day to do my exercises at Harry Abrahams' gym. That was where Reggie and Ronnie used to go to do their sparring, because they were useful boxers. They were only 17 then, and I'd sit on the edge of the ring, watching them sparring; and then they'd watch me lifting the weights. Afterwards we'd go off, drink coffee or go down to the Grave Maurice pub, and then we might go back to their Mum's place in Vallance Road for a meal or have a game of cards, playing 11–4 rummy. The twins both had a left and a right, which was unusual. When I used to come up here to Leicester Square, they would come up with me and could they perform! That was before the blades came out. All they done was knuckles, fist fights. If anyone was naughty, they'd say, 'All right, son!' – and then, smack! Being two-handers, they could switch from south paw to the right, and back again, without warning, but they didn't want to become professional boxers because then you get a broken nose or a cauliflower ear and they wanted to stay sharp. They didn't want to mess their features up, and to this day neither of them has a scar and neither of them has been cut with a blade. If anyone ever cut me on the boat race, I'd kill 'em. And I mean it. I'd kill 'em.

They had one fight at the Royal Albert Hall, but I missed that one, although I saw them fight a few times down at the baths in Cambridge Heath Road. They weren't villains then. That came later, after they'd come back from doing their National Service, although the 'firm' was starting to take shape, even then. They got court-martialled for going absent without leave and for striking an officer, and I went down to see them in the military prisons at Colchester and Shepton Mallet. Not only me; they had plenty of friends, but it was hard for us to get into gaol, usually, although I could get away with it easier than the others. The Colchester nick was between Aldham and Colchester, and they banged Ronnie up in one wing and Reggie in another. They wouldn't let them stick together. I was allowed five minutes with them, top whack, to have a chat, sitting in front of a wire cage, but that was enough for them to give me a message to pass on to other members of the 'firm'. I was only allowed to get away with it because of my size. It's just because I'm little, and when I need to do it I'm a groveller because I know that's what the fuckers want. When I put my mind to it I can get away with anything. The 'firm' was still in its very early days, just working around the East End before we moved up West.

Chapter 4

When I first knew Reggie and Ronnie Kray they never used to drink very much. That was just after my first visit to the United States. They had jobs in those days, working for a tailor's down the East End, and they were more interested in their boxing than villainy. I used to travel with them around the East End. Down Mile End, I once saw them step into the ring together. That was the night Ronnie knocked Reggie out in two rounds, and shortly after that I went with them down to Ilford when they had a bare-knuckle fight in the Green Park, just for fun.

Then a fellow called Roy Shaw came up with the idea that they should raise money for charity, and they were having these bare-knuckle fights, with blood all over the place. That was on Ilford Green, too. Large crowds came down to watch them. There was betting, and they used to have someone with what we called 'the shoe', walking through the crowd collecting money. They raised a lot of money that way for charity.

By that time I was living in St Stephen's Crescent, Paddington, with this singer Heddy Horden, whom I met touring the halls. She came from Sunderland, and one week she might be working in one town and me in another, but when we were 'resting', as they say in our business, we had this tiny flat, not much bigger than a bedsitter, where I lived, on and off, for years. She was a good kid, and it might have lasted, but even then I had a drink problem and was doing what they call 'speeding' now; I was taking Preludin pills with gin, and that would give me a lift. I've never been able to go out on stage, out on a job, or even up a flight of stairs, unless I've had a drop of dustman's courage, but I didn't start taking the whisky until I was well into my twenties. Then it was gin, and I started taking the pills when I did a short variety tour with the Billy Cotton Band Show. His singer, Alan Breeze, used to have a very bad stutter, and he was on Bennies (Benzedrine) which were a bit too heavy for me because of the drink, but that was how I started the pills.

I did a lot of variety, working with Anne Shelton, Vera Lynn, Jimmy Wheeler, Max Miller – we called him 'Sequin Joe' – and Old Mother Riley, Arthur Lucan, who was a poofter. How Kitty McShane ever married him, I shall never know, but she was a drinker and used to go out drinking with the drummer in the orchestra.

You always have periods when you're not working in show business, but with me I never stopped; when I got back to London, I would be out busking or working my fruit barrows, anything so long as I had money of my own. I started my first fruit barrow in Great Newport Street, near Leicester Square station, in the late forties, and must have had barrows for nearly thirty years; when I was out touring, or banged up in the nick, I'd have what we call 'bucks' working the barrows for me. As well as that one at Great Newport Street, which was a 'show barrow', all nice and tidy with a good display of fruit, I had others in Bear Street and, later, in Argyll Street, close to the London Palladium. There was a lot of money in fruit barrows in those days, but the stuffing was knocked out of the trade when the old Covent Garden market closed and the wholesalers moved down to Nine Elms, and the Weights and Measures inspectors are very strict these days.

I used to do all the buying myself at first, but I became so well known, eventually, that I could always send someone up to Covent Garden to buy all me fruit. There were so many 'cons' in that game.

On the scales, we used to have two half-crowns tied underneath what we called the jigger, and that would load the scales a couple of ounces in our favour; or, alternatively, we would have a couple of half-crowns on one side of the scales, tucked inside a paper bag with the weight permanently on the scale so that the punters would never know it didn't balance. All those two ounces made a big difference by the end of the day. When we made a show on the stall, all the big strawberries would go at the front and all the wet ones behind, and then the trick was to have two paper bags, one inside the other, so that the wet wouldn't come through too quick. By the time the punters get up the road, the bags might be wet, but they're not likely to come back. Cherries were terrible. When they go mouldy they sweat and go hot and can burn your hand; it's hard work handling cherries.

Another trick was to always have your little finger resting on the scales as you were weighing the fruit, and you were safer doing that than altering the weights because, even then, the Weights and Measures inspectors would still come round sometimes and check them, always looking inside your brass weights which were hollow to see if you'd added a little extra lead. At the side of your barrow, you'd have your bags ready so that you just had to top them up when the punters came along; there'd be a rotten banana or loose grapes in the bottom of the bag, and you'd let them watch you pop in ripe bananas or a little bunch of grapes and then say, 'Thank you very much, sir,' as they walked away with a load of shit. I know it was wicked, but that was where you made your profit.

I was always restless, and when I'd got money in my pocket I'd be off down the East End, with a 'buck' working the barrow, and then I might not go down to the gym for a week or two if I had a theatre booking or a little bit of business, but I'd try to get down there if I could because I was building up my muscles and when Reggie and Ronnie were youngsters they couldn't get over me. I don't think they ever really set out to go on the wrong side of the law, but once they got into running clubs there was a lot of jealousy. That was what it was like down the East End. There was always one firm trying to knock out another firm, and if you were going to survive you had to prove that you could do the business, and even if you thought you were going straight, you could still get your arm twisted.

The thing with the Krays was that we always had a place to meet, and that was what made it, really; we were all good friends. Joe Abrahams had that gym first and then his son Harry took it over when Joe died. Harry has now got the 81 Club on Stepney Green, just as you turn left out of Stepney Green station. Another meeting place we had was the Prince of Wales pub, which was just around the corner from the gym, and then we moved on to the Grave Maurice, which was where we met for years, long after Reggie and Ronnie started running clubs of their own. I knew that I could drive over there any morning, and I'd always be welcome.

That affair with Heddy lasted a couple of years, but she didn't like me mixing the pills and the drink and going off so much, and in the end she went back home to Sunderland and married a guy who was secretary of a working men's club. He was a very placid sort of a guy, not like me; some years later I was working up there and went round to see her. By then, she had three sons, and she came out to the car and sat and talked to me for a bit. 'It could have worked,' she said, but it didn't, and that's it.

I still carried on living at the flat in St Stephen's Crescent and was there when Timothy Evans was topped. He and Christie were living just around the corner in Rillington Place, and I remember reading in the papers how Christie had gone to court and given evidence against him. I used to see Christie around the streets after that, four-eyed, but he seemed such a nice old boy. You would never have dreamt that he was killing all those women. He was only a small man, and when I met him in the street he would raise his hat and say 'Good morning' and then I'd say 'Good morning', and then I'd see him around the cafés in Notting Hill and Paddington and he'd always have a few words to say. When they topped him, I was in the Scrubs.

The first time I went to the United States was in 1948 or 1949. I was trying to make myself scarce after that business at Slough, and when my agent, Kay Lester, who used to represent all the dwarfs and midgets, told me that I could get work out there as a midget wrestler, I jumped at the chance. I went from Southampton on a French boat, and then transferred to one of the Cunard liners a few miles out, arriving in New York with an address to go to, money in my pocket, and a three-month visa. When we docked we had to go through Customs and all that shit, with me carrying just one small suitcase, but I got a steward to carry that for me; people will always help you when you're little.

Out there I used to mimic the wrestler Gorgeous George, who was a great star on the wrestling circuit. I had my hair dyed blond and I used to have this little pig, which I dyed blond as well. Cor, did it scream – 'cos I used peroxide bleach.

I used to arrive in town on promotion, ahead of the other wrestlers, with my blond hair flowing down my back and dressed in silks and sequins, with this pig walking behind me on a lead. Then I would strut into the biggest restaurants in town and say, in my best, poshest, most exaggerated English accent, 'I'd like a nice cup of tea mixed with a spot of coffee.' They would look at me as if I was mad, while I'd stand there ignoring them, preening myself in front of the mirror (there were always lots of mirrors in those sort of restaurants), looking from side to side at my profile, flexing my muscles and combing my hair, and then when the waitress came back, I would ask for a large bourbon. When she brought it, I would pour the bourbon into the tea and hand it to the pig, saying, 'Now this is swill . . .', and without them seeing me I'd give him a little kick to make sure he squealed. By this time, everyone in the restaurant would have stopped eating, and they would all be looking at me wondering what was going to happen next. I'd still be talking to the pig: 'Now you shut up . . . or I'll eat your trotters!'

There were three other midget wrestlers on the tour, Tiny Tim, Sky Lolo and Little Beaver, and as it happens that was unfortunate because Sky Lolo strangled Little Beaver in a row over a woman down in Mobile, Alabama, and that brought the tour to an abrupt end. They didn't put him in prison. He was sent to a psychiatric hospital instead. Little people are often possessive, especially over women. They have this big chip on their shoulders, and they say, 'That's mine, that's mine, that's mine,' but I don't. I love them and leave them.

When I came back to London, I introduced midget wrestling to England. That was in 1949, and for many years after that, in between the pantos, variety, the fruit stalls and the odd bit of villainy, I'd turn my hand to wrestling when there was some good money to be had.

I had three promoters – Paul Lincoln, Judo Al Hayes, and then the one I dealt with last, Mike Merino. Now, you gotta understand that wrestling is bent, and I mean BENT! That's professional wrestling; amateur wrestling is different. Then you've really got to squeeze and throw, but in professional wrestling you learn how to do holds like the Irish Whip, the Headmare, the Nelson Body Slam and the Claw in such a way that no one gets hurt, and some wrestlers used to have gelatine pills made up specially, containing Ribena, so that they could take a bite and get the 'blood' flowing in the ring. I used to have a piece of razor blade tucked away in my body belt where it could never hurt me, and then between rounds I'd give myself a nick in the eyebrow, which would get the blood flowing down my face, which is what the punters want to see; they want blood, especially with someone like me because I was always a 'baddie'.

For years I had my own tag team, with three other little fellers, so that we could travel round the country putting on our own tag team contests wherever we went. I was always the guvnor and paid the wages. I'd pick up a long 'un (£100) for a night's work and then give 'em each twelve quid. The rest was all mine – and I always picked up the travelling expenses as well. We never earned less than a long 'un, and sometimes a good bit more. I had two brothers working with me. One of them was good looking and could do the air spins, and the other looked a villain, just like me, and had a cauliflower ear. He had made it himself, 'cos he thought that would make him look better for the part; you always have to have a nice guy and a bad guy in every wrestling match because, again, that's what the punters like, and when these wrestlers want to give themselves a cauliflower ear they just take out a spoon, put it behind the ear and pump the lobe of the ear to make the blood come out, and then it stays like that for ever. I've seen it done many times, but I've never done it myself because I'm ugly enough without it; they think it makes 'em look good, just like some people like to wear a scar, or to be tattooed.

We had some great times wrestling. I used to go out on the road with Mick McManus, Jackie Pallo, the Cortez brothers, Mike Merino, Judo Al Hayes, and one of my really good mates, Sky High Lee, who first came over from Texas while I was out in the States for the first time. We used to cause a big stir when we walked down Old Compton Street together because Sky High was 6ft 10in. tall, and I'm only 4ft 2in., and he used to exaggerate his height still further by wearing his Texan gear – jeans, big leather belt, high-heeled boots with spurs, check shirts and a ten-gallon stetson – and I'd be walking along beside him, dressed the same way. Sky High was a bit thick but I liked the guy; he was the same as me, liked whisky and garlic, and when we were going out on the road we'd meet all the other wrestlers at the Parkway Restaurant in Camden Town, where we'd have an egg on toast and a whisky before we went off in the minibus. We had certain times when we would meet. If we were only going to Birmingham, we didn't have to meet until twelve o'clock midday, but if it was Blackpool, then we'd meet a bit earlier, say 10.30.

At that time, American wrestlers could only come here to work for forty nights under the immigration laws that were then in force, and so we tumbled that there was a way of getting round this. I introduced him to this little bird and said to him, 'Why don't you get married?' Now, she was a brass, a prostitute, a wrong 'un, but I told him this didn't matter. All he had to do was get her down to the register office, get that piece of paper signed, give her a bit of bread, and then it would be 'Bye-bye, baby'. As long as you've got that piece of paper, and you're married to a British citizen, you're here. Well, he pays her a grand (£1,000), and I took a few quid, because business is business, and then she marries him and he never sees her again.

One night we were wrestling in Ireland. Now, although Sky was a strong man we all knew that he couldn't work too hard. He couldn't take the body slams or the whips, so it had to be forearm smash or grabbing by the hair, which is easy, doesn't hurt. This night, Sky gets disqualified, which had all been rehearsed beforehand in the dressing room, but this geezer in the audience got so excited by the 'fight' that he jumped into the ring, all dressed in a blue suit. I can see him now. He took off his jacket to give Sky High one, but there was the other wrestler, the seconds and the referee all standing in his way, so he tried to kick Sky High in the balls instead. Sky High wasn't having that, and thumped his fist down on the geezer's head, which was like being hit with a 28lb hammer. Down he went out cold. The ambulancemen came and took him to hospital, where he died, and then the Garda came round and questioned us all. Sky High wasn't charged. The Garda accepted that it had been an accident and that the other guy was to blame, but when Sky High came back to

London he started drinking more heavily than ever, and it soon got to the stage where he was too ill to wrestle. He was always drinking, day in and day out, but not like me. I always take just a sip at a time but he was pouring it down his throat until, in the end, he was dead, poor sod. And do you know, he never, ever, got his leg over; not once, not even with that girl who cost him a grand.

You often find that wrestlers die suddenly. There was another good mate of mine, Mike Merino, who used to teach young ladies to wrestle down at Gravesend, and then opened the Queens in Rhyl. He died suddenly, too. It was a heart attack, and I'll probably go the same way.

My biggest mate in wrestling was Tommy Gallagher, whom I discovered and trained myself. I was driving along the Commercial Road in my car and saw him loading a fruit lorry; stopped the car, introduced myself, and asked him if he wouldn't like to make a bit more money. He couldn't read or write in those days, but I taught him the wrestling game in four Saturdays, working out at the old Metropole in the Edgware Road, and then took him out on the road. I dressed him in green and called him Tiny Tim, the Wee Leprechaun from Eire, and myself, Fuzzyball Kaye from the USA, still wearing the long hair and the flowing cape, just like I'd done in the States, always stepping into the ring looking very conceited, so that the crowd would boo and hiss, hoping that Tommy would win. We stayed together for years, until he fell in love one night in Newcastle; he brought the girl to meet me, with her coat held together with a safety pin, and I knew that wouldn't last, which it didn't. He's still a friend of mine and I see him now and again; he's working at the Opera House in Covent Garden, polishing the brass.

I am very fortunate because I could always turn to wrestling, the pantos, and other work, because I had never been bandy like most dwarfs. My legs go sometimes now as I'm getting on in years and there's rheumatism and arthritis in the joints, but I'm not bandy, and that's down to my mother. Most dwarfs are bandy because their legs can't take the body weight, but I'm not like that. I can stand to attention, and that's down to my mother because when she saw that my legs were small when I was a baby, she exercised me, which is what I did with my own daughter. She used to lift me up and then wrap tapes or bandages around my legs so that they wouldn't go bandy, and the leg muscles grew used to bearing the weight. It's the same as gypsies always know how to lay their babies down to sleep so that their ears are tucked in properly. Here (at the St Mungo hostel), you see blokes with their ears sticking out from the sides of their heads, and that's because their mothers didn't lay them down properly as babies; if you're a gypsy you know the score. You know what herbs to use in the country instead of medicines. My mother was always boiling up the stinging nettles, for the animals as well as for us, and then she would throw in other herbs as well so that the dogs were never ill, and neither were the horses. We never used medicines but ate natural foods, fruit and vegetables, hazel nuts, bilberries, cockles and mussels, whatever was going.

Before I left for America the second time, Mum told me that Dad had lung cancer and was going to die. He had had one lung taken out, and in those days once one lung went, the other went. 'Dad,' I said, 'I am going to leave you. I've gotta go.' Mum, God rest her soul, didn't try to stop me, and neither did my brothers or sisters, and soon after I had arrived in the States I heard that he had died in her arms. They used to row terribly because of the drink and him coming home pissed, but she loved him and sometimes she would go out looking for him, afraid that he might have fallen under a bus, and then she'd bring him home. I loved them both, and when I heard that he had passed away I didn't want to talk to anyone. That was when I became a really bad boy.

Kay Lester had got me a job working in the King Brothers' Circus, but once I was over there it was the old, old story. I was into everything. I met this Yankee Johnny, who was really an English boy, but he had an American accent, and he says, 'Are you game?' Of course, I was game. Together we went out working the doors; that's when you do the big hotels. First, you go down into the lounge to find out who are the Champagne Charlies, and which rooms they are staying in. Then you go round the corridors, find their rooms, and nick their wallets. Sometimes we were unlucky. Other times we scored. We made a lot of money, working our way across the States with the circus, always going from hotel to hotel in every town. We call that 'fingering', and it's a good game. If you're captured, you just have to give the police a good talking to, and weigh them in a little bit here and there. Most policemen are bent, and a little bit of dropsy will get you out of trouble every time.

Once I got accused of taking a lady's handbag, which is something I have never done, and a suede coat, and once they'd captured me the police also told me I had robbed a jeweller's, which I had. 'Let's have a little talk,' I said, and that solved the problem. Usually, you only have to pay £50 or £100, or a nice round sum in dollars. The most I have ever had to pay was £800, which was when I had done a big blag, a naughty one, pushing a guy down upon his arse; I'd known he had the money because he had just come out of a bank. I can't remember how much he had, but even after paying off the police, it was still worth doing.

That second tour of America taught me a hell of a lot. Different con-games. How to make a nickel. I met a lot of villains, and when we were on the road they always used to give me good introductions, so that when we hit a new town I always had the address of a good place to go to.

In New York City, I used to hang out at Jack Dempsey's place. Although it was a restaurant, there was also a long bar where many of the New York villains used to meet. Jack used to stand at the bar with Joe Louis, some nights, and later gave him a job when he had no bread. Joe was out of the game, a fool with money, but a lovely guy. I met him several times. I was never a big eater, and just went down there for a drink and to meet the boys. It was a meeting place like the Grave Maurice, and every city had one. In Boston, Massachusetts, we used to meet at Danny's Bar, and at Sarasota in Florida, it was the Circus Lounge, where a lot of the Mafia boys used to hang out, and there were others in Chicago and New Orleans, whose names I've forgotten. It was like Britain; there were different firms in every town or city, but they'd always make you welcome if you had an introduction. I met a lot of show business people over there as well, especially when I started getting little jobs in films. I was in the film *Trapeze* with Burt Lancaster, and *Circus* with Kirk Douglas, but had to pull out of *The Greatest Show on Earth,* which starred John Wayne, after hurting myself bad.

In that movie I was due to film a midget wrestling scene, and was all dressed up in my cape, standing at the side of the ring. On the other side of the ring were two chimpanzees, both wearing boxing gloves; they were as big as me, maybe a bit bigger, and they'd been filmed doing a boxing routine. Well, they took one look at me and shot across the ring, and hit me with their fists, BANG, BANG, BANG! Their handlers pulled them off, and it may seem funny, but I couldn't walk for days.

I made another film in Virginia called *The Terror from Tiny Town,* in which all the actors were midgets and everything else was normal size. I was the Terror, and in one scene I had to burst into a Wild West bar and shoot a hole in a paper cup with my Colt 45. Someone had already stuck a pencil through the cup to make the hole, but as the cup went flying in the air I had to fire the shot, and then as the crowd ran to pick up the cup, they all went 'Ooooooh!' and 'Aaaaagh!' and I had the big lines, 'Now, who wants me?' It was all great fun.

On a golf course in Florida, I met Frank Sinatra, and also Dean Martin and the other with the squeaky voice, Jerry Lewis. Down at Daytona Beach, I was introduced to Bing Crosby and his wife, and in Connecticut, Paul Newman.

I loved the United States. Everyone was very kind to me, but I soon realised that the Mafia were very close to show business. In those days, it was all down to protection. The Mafia had some cities completely tied up, and if you didn't do as they told you then you were brown bread. At the same time, they looked after you and treated you as one of their own. One night I was in Johnny Walker's bar on Fifth Avenue when two guys walked in. I recognised one of them [name deleted] straight away. Even then, he was a big Hollywood star and he was with this group of Mafia men, all suited and booted. I had already met them, and one of them said to me later, 'He's gotta have a talking to,' and it was quite clear who was the boss. If you become a star, the Mafia will tell you what to do and where to go – and if you don't go along with it, you're sacked. George Raft was another of the guys I met in New York, and he was a real Jack the Lad; never had any money, but was always hanging around the bars with the boys. Some years later, Ronnie and Reggie wanted to bring him over to act as a host at their club, the El Morocco, and we all had a whip-round to raise £4,000 for his expenses. But when the boys went out to Heathrow airport the authorities wouldn't let George into the country because of his Mafia connections.

None of that surprised me because I'd been there in the fifties, met them and seen it all for myself.

I had gone over there originally on a three-month visa, travelling this time on the *Mauretania*. That was when I met Tommy Steele. He was like a service boy. You rang a buzzer and he came. I met him on the deck during his tea breaks when I'd gone up there feeling seasick. He was sitting there, playing his guitar and we got talking. As soon as I heard his voice, I said to him, 'You're a Londoner. Don't tell me. I bleeding know – you're Bermondsey, aint yer?' He told me he wanted to go into show business. 'I think I'll make it,' he said.

'Don't build castles in the air,' I told him, but he did it, didn't he? He asked me if I'd like a nice bit of supper put on one side for me, but I says, 'No, give us one of them birds...', because the *Mauretania* was full of these GI brides setting off for America.

Kay Lester had got me this job with King Brothers' Circus, paying 120 US dollars a week, which was good money in those days. I used to be a good tumbler, and also had a high diving act where I climbed up a 40ft ladder and then dived head first into what was said to be a 5ft deep tank of water, although actually it was 8ft. There was a trick to that, like everything else. You had to dive with your hands outstretched so that your fingers touched the bottom of the tank, and then, provided you did that, you would turn in the water and come back to the top. Easy. But if you didn't, then your head might hit the bottom and you could get killed.

Although I'd only got a three-month visa, I stayed in the States for nearly four years before getting captured. And those were wonderful years. I had some fabulous times.

When I was staying at Tampa, Florida, I met this sheriff; a huge feller, with a belly bulging out of his uniform over his trousers and with a gun in his belt.

'Shorty, do you wanna come and have a ride with me?' he says, with this southern drawl.

'Where are you going?'

'The Everglades.'

'What are we going to do there?'

'We're gonna get some moonshine, boy!'

So we drove from Tampa down through St Petersburg

and the Silverglades to the Everglades, until we came to a point where the sheriff says, 'Shorty, this is where we've gotta get in the canoe.'

'What are we gonna do?' I says, because now we're right on the edge of the swamp.

'We're just gonna go through there, and then we're gonna have a little walk,' he says.

'I'm game,' I said, but as we were going through the swamp in this canoe there were crocodiles coming up close, snapping their jaws, and that was too much for me. I didn't like that. My bottle went. The sheriff had his shooter, but I hadn't got one and I didn't feel safe at all, with these trees hanging down low over the water and all those crocodiles.

'How much further have we gotta go?'

'Another fifteen minutes.'

Blimey, it was shaking me, but I wasn't letting him know that, and then, all of a sudden, the trees opened out and there was this fucking great distillery right in the middle of the swamp with all these blacks working there, and the sheriff just stands there chewing his tobacco which is something I couldn't suffer. When the blacks saw me they freaked out. I mean, I'm a white man with little legs, and they've never seen anything like it before. While they're loading up the canoe for us to go back, this big black guy picked me up in his arms like a baby and put me in the canoe. Now, all this was illegal. The sheriff was breaking the law and making moonshine was a crime, and here am I, in the middle of a swamp, surrounded by crocodiles. As we got back to the motor, the sheriff must have seen that I was worried 'cos he says, 'Are you all right boy?'

'Yeah, I'm all right,' I said, but then I said, 'Thank God for that,' to myself when we got back to the motor, 'cos I hadn't felt safe at all.

'You want some of this?' he says, offering me some of the moonshine bourbon. Then as we're driving along in the car, he says, 'Let me cut you in on this' – and gives me ten dollars, which was a nice sum of money thirty-five years ago. 'You just hang on in there, boy,' he said, "cos I like you, and I'm gonna introduce you to a lot of people,' and he did, too, because Americans love to hear a Cockney accent. He took me round the supermarkets and the clubs, and wherever we went people were giving me presents.

Also down in Tampa, I went into a bar and met this guy called Chuck Arenth who had a physical training school with two gymnasiums. There was one for the guys and one for those old girls with money who came in wearing their hot pants to do their exercises, with the old vibrators strapped around their bums so that they can lose weight, or riding on exercise bikes, going boom, boom, boom. Chuck was into carrot juice and all that stuff.

There was a guy called Paul Anderson, a big fat American, with great fat legs, so large that he had to waddle like Japanese Sumo wrestlers. He thought he was so powerful as he worked away at the squats, the curls and the lifts – which are the basic things you have to do in weight-lifting – before doing the bench-press.

Now, with the bench-press you have to lie down on your back on a form with the weights up there above you on the rack, and then when you take them off you *must*, the first thing you do, open your mouth and take a deep breath, and then you can let the breath out as you push up. Big fat Paul Anderson forgot to breathe in, and the weights fell across his neck. We had to lift them off, because otherwise he would have been dead.

There were all these guys lifting up the weights, and in walks Marlon Brando. Now, I'm going back to the days when he was fit, at the beginning of his career in movies. I didn't know who he was, but Chuck Arenth knew him well, and Brando stood there, watching me lifting these 56lb weights, one in each hand.

'You're OK,' he says.

'So are you!'

'Where are you from?'

'Isn't it obvious, with my bleeding accent?' And then I gave him a jab, because I didn't take shit from anyone in those days. In those days I used to lift the weights, do squats, and show off me muscles, and because I've got short arms and those extra strong biceps, I could handle much heavier weights than anyone would ever think I could.

'What do you do, boy?' says Brando.

'Not a lot.'

'What are you doing in this country?'

'I didn't come here to see you.'

Chuck Arenth could see that I was getting riled, with him calling me 'Boy' and all that, and gave him the whisper; told him that I was a midget wrestler, a weight-lifter, and worked in the circus, and he looked me up and down, nodding his head, thinking about it.

'Are you happy?'

'Well, sometimes,' I says. 'When I work with Snow White and the Seven Dwarfs, I'm Happy, but when someone upsets me, I'm Grumpy – and no one would ever call me Dopey . . .'

I want to go to the bar now, don't I, 'cos I've had enough of this kind of talking, and Brando walks over there with me and tells me he's making this film *The Wild One*, and asks me whether I would like to have a part in it. 'You don't think I'm an extra, do yer?' I said to him. I wasn't having that. There was good money coming through from the circus, and all the other little things I had going, so I didn't need it, did I?

On the King Brothers' Circus, there were ten girl dancers, which wasn't a lot; later, when I worked on the Ringland Brothers, Barnum and Bailey Circus, there were forty dancers, but of those ten I had three working for me in every town. I was poncing, and that brought more money in. I was doing well.

When the circus rode into a new town, there would always be a parade to let the townspeople know we had arrived, and I would be right up there, sitting on the elephant's head or riding bareback on a pony, and then there would be a crowd while the tent was erected. First, they would put up the big poles in the middle, which we called the king poles; then the four queen poles would go up around the ring, and then, lastly, the jacks, which are the poles around the edge of the tent, and we'd have all the dossers and layabouts running about, putting those up for a bottle of wine, which was why we called them the jumping jacks. And then when the tent had to come down, I would take charge, paying all the kiddies nickels and dimes. Small change. No US dollars. I was always the paymaster 'cos I would go to the guvnor and say, 'Leave this to me. I'll sort this out.' Then with a bucket of small change I'd get the kids packing up the show, and I'd have the elephants moving the king poles and the queens; there were thirteen elephants, all girls but for one bull, and they'd do anything for me.

There was one elephant, Mola, who used to come to me if I called her. She knew my voice, and she worked for me because she knew I would never hurt her. I used to have a walking stick with a bent nail on the end, which wasn't spiteful because their skins are so thick that they can only feel a prick. The thing to do with an elephant is to give them a prick behind the ears or on their front feet, and then they will come walkies. I was always very gentle, and Mola would do anything for me.

When we moved from town to town, she and the other elephants travelled in big trucks. There were fifteen or sixteen trucks, and we travelled in convoy, which was an advertisement in itself. There were two trucks with ponies, and then others with bears, chimpanzees, lions, giraffes, camels, tigers, every mortal animal. You name it, they had it. I sat on one of those camels once, and my bum was bleeding aching after that. The ones with the two humps were all right, because you could sit in the middle; but the ones with one hump were painful.

One way and another, with the little bits of villainy that I had going on the side, I reckoned that I was making 400 US dollars a week, and that was good money for the early fifties. I was having a great time, and never short of women.

Down in Macon, Georgia, there's a big US Air Force base called Warner Robbins, and the King Brothers' Circus stayed down there for three weeks. Georgia was a dry state, but they had what they called 'out-door,' which was like an off-licence, where you could pick up packs of Budweiser or Schlitz beers, and then bring them back into the cubicles where they served Seven-Up and Coca-Cola. No one seemed to mind, and the night we hit town this barmaid, Phyllis, came to my cubicle, and said, 'Are you English?'

'Well, sort of – I'm British.'

'Are you working with the King Brothers' Circus?'

'I will be when it starts.'

'Where are you staying?'

I told her that we had only just arrived and that I was looking for a motel.

'I think you're cute,' she says, and at first she wanted me to go back to her place for the night. Well, I played hard to get, and asked her whether she had a telly and how far we had to go, whether she could lay me on some scranny, and if she had a wee dram for me to drink.

'We'll soon fix that,' she says, calls a taxi, books us into a room for the night, goes and has a shower, and then she comes back, jumps into bed and does the business, sweet as a nut.

'I think I'm in love with you,' she says.

'You silly cow,' I told her. 'How can you be in love with me? Look at me. I'm a dwarf. I'm a little guy, and you've only just met me. How can you be in love with me? But I'd love to stay with you,' and I did, all the time we were in

Macon, and then when the time came for the circus to move on, the tears came. She didn't want me to go. Crying, she was. 'What's the matter with you?' I said. 'I've gotta go. I can't stay here. There's no money for me here. I've gotta get to work . . .'

'Will you come back?' she says.

'Time will tell,' I told her. 'Time will tell.'

Chapter 5

Those American adventures came to an end when the immigration authorities captured me without a visa, and I was deported. That was in the winter of 1957. It was my fault for being careless, and I might still be there now if they hadn't caught me, but I had had a good run, having gone to the States on a three-month visa and then stayed for nearly four years.

My mistake was falling in with a guy called Kennedy, an American boy whose father was what we called a butcher, someone who sells novelties, Coca-Cola, ice cream or candy floss. We met down at Daytona Beach in Florida. I had left the King Brothers' Circus, and was going off on tour with the Ringland Brothers, Barnum and Bailey Circus, instead. By then I was hustling, making good money, and this guy Kennedy says, 'Why don't we go down to Havana for the weekend?' This was on a Friday night. He says, 'The women won't cost you nothing; just wine and dine 'em.' So I was game. We went down to the airport, boarded a plane, and within an hour we were there. This is Havana in Cuba. When we arrive, Kennedy calls a taxi, and takes me to this hotel. It was bleeding warm.

'I've gotta have a wee dram,' I tells him, and all of a sudden this little girl comes over, sits down, and says, 'You're cute!'

'Yeah, I'm all right,' I says. 'How are you?'

'Do you like me?' she says.

'Yeah. Tasty, aren't yer?'

'I like your accent,' she says, speaking like half-Mexican, Cuban, broken English, as this mate of mine comes back and says, 'Is she all right?'

'Yeah, sweet as a nut,' I says, as he tells me he has booked me a room.

'Do you want to talk to me?' she says.

'You bet,' I said, as we went upstairs, stripped off, had a shower, a kiss and a cuddle, and did the biz. Me? I'm stupid. I should have flown back to Daytona Beach on the Monday, and then there would have been no problem, but I got carried away and spent ten days with her. She was lovely, and when I got back to Daytona Beach they captured me. Picked me up at the airport, found I had no visa and took my passport, and then put me on a Greyhound bus back to New York City with a policeman guarding me. Had I been tall, they would have handcuffed me, but they let me sit on the bus without cuffs when they realised that I couldn't run anywhere with my legs. 'You're going home. You know that, don't you?' they said, even though I had a lot of dough, and I mean *a lot*, on me. When they got me to New York City, they took me to a hotel on Eighth Avenue, and it was a pisser, worse than a dosshouse.

'How have you been managing?' says the British Consul, thinking I've got no money and have been out of the game. I'm loaded with money, but that's not what they think when they pick up someone like me without a visa, so he gives me twenty dollars' pocket money to cover my bed and grub. Well, I don't want to stay in this poxy bughouse so I slips the receptionist five dollars and tells him that he can use the room for brasses, prostitutes, overnight, and that I'll be back in the morning to change.

'Thank you very much, man,' he says, and I know where I'm going, because I know New York City like the back of my bleeding hand, and comes back at nine o'clock in the morning, just to have a shower and change my shirt, because in them days I was suited and booted. Then I goes back to see the Consul who tells me he has booked me back to Britain on the *Mauretania* and gives me another twenty dollars, although I'm still carrying a lot of bleeding dough, easily 1,600 dollars.

The boat was supposed to leave at eleven o'clock on the

Saturday morning, and they escorted me to the pier and handed my passport over to the Purser, who takes me down to the bar and buys me a drink. 'You're an entertainer, aren't you?' And I ends up being *paid* to entertain the passengers, working with a group of black musicians, singing all that old Bing Crosby–Frank Sinatra stuff, and playing my old girl (his ukelele), and being given one of the best cabins. I got the real VIP treatment, and when we got back to Southampton the Captain and the Purser both shook my hand, and said, 'There's only the two of us that know you have been deported . . .' Then I went to stay with my sister Helen and her husband Dick Crossley, God rest his soul, who owned the Basset Arms Hotel, not far from Southampton. He had been captain of a ship and later died of cancer of the throat, and there I got a hero's welcome 'cos everyone thought I'd gone missing. I'd only said that I was going for the three months, and they hadn't heard from me since. I'd never written or phoned, or even sent a card.

I comes back to London, sees my mother, calls on Kay Lester, who soon finds me work in a touring revue, *The Best Years of Your Lives*, and quickly gets back into the swing of things, although I hear that while I have been away Ronnie has been arrested and gaoled for three years for causing grievous bodily harm, and while he's been banged up Reggie had opened the Double R Club in Bow Road, Bethnal Green. As soon as he hears I'm back in town, which, of course, he does, Reggie phones me up and asks me to go down there in the evenings as a sort of social thing, to keep him company, and that brought me back on the firm. There wasn't too much thieving, more the con, the tweedle and the twirl, but when they put a bit of business my way, I'd weigh them in, but not too heavy.

Whatever happens, I'm at it, and there's always money coming in from somewhere. If I'm not wrestling, I'm in panto, touring in variety, getting the odd part in films – I was in the film *Beau Brummel* with Elizabeth Taylor and

Michael Wilding – or going back to my fruit barrows, never 'resting'.

Kay Lester was good to me, always keeping in touch, even when I was in the nick, and she found me a lot of work. She used to have an office at 29 Burleigh Mansions in the Charing Cross Road, and lived there as well with a girl called Kathy, a midget, whose Mum and Dad had chucked her out of the door. Kathy was a little bit simple and the one thing she wanted, above all else, was boobs, because she kept seeing these girls coming into the office who all had good ones. That was the worst thing she ever done, having the injections, because she got the breasts but they went all floppy.

Kay Lester was my agent for about twelve years. It was she who introduced me to midget wrestling, the King Brothers' Circus, and then the Ringland Brothers, Barnum and Bailey Circus. She was an old-style Jewish agent, who had been around, and earned her 10 per cent. The firm had started in America as John Lester's Midgets, and then Kay had opened an office in London as well so they could find us work in both countries. She represented most of the midgets who were working in show business, and had fourteen or fifteen on her books. I think I got more work than most of them because she always knew where to find me; my fruit barrows in Bear Street and Great Newport Street were very close to her office.

The one time when I worked with a lot of other dwarfs and midgets was when she booked us into the Festival of Britain in 1951, in between my two American tours. We worked there for eight months, running a Toy Town sideshow, and then took it to Belle Vue, Manchester. That was a good money-spinner. You couldn't miss it, right under the Wall of Death, the motorbikes, and, being me, I ended up half running the show. Once I had taught Georgie Craven, another dwarf, to use the microphone, I only had to pop down there to see them for an hour or so a day; Georgie's a nice little fellow, but shrewd. Works for a travel agency now.

We were up to all sorts of tricks. Every morning I would go out and buy a tray of sausage rolls and sandwiches, and then I'd slice them up into little bits, and put them on tiny plates. That was 'food for the little people'. Then we had postcards on sale so that people could send a postcard from Toy Town, with our own postbox, and the Post Office used to send a van round to collect it. We also had the smallest married couple which was Dorothy Williams and Freddie Carlisle, who used to work with Harry Lester and the Hayseeds. Dorothy is still alive. She's about 3ft 2in. and lives down at Herne Hill. Freddie is about 3ft 10in. As you came in the door, there was another midget driving a motor car, a mini-Austin run off a battery, and then I also installed a Wishing Well, and couldn't go wrong with that. We used to have to scoop out the money at the end of every day; there was a plug in the bottom, which the punters couldn't see, and we'd just empty the well, scoop up the money, and then fill it up with water again before we opened the next morning.

I was paying all their wages, and then taking the takings from the 'Ding', standing on the door with a microphone, saying 'Walk right in, ladies and gentlemen. Walk right in. There are no tickets. Just walk in the door. Everyone welcome. Walk right in . . .' and then as they came in through the door, I gave them all a lucky horseshoe, which was the old gypsy trick, and said 'Thank you very much' as they dropped their coins into the tin, which was why we always call it 'The Ding', because that's the noise it makes.

When we took the show to Manchester, Charlie Forte (now Lord Forte) gave me the sack. He tumbled how much money I was making after I had weighed them all in, and he had this list. This one gets £5 a week, that one £6, that one £7, and realised how much must have been coming from 'The Ding'. The greedy little bugger put a cashbox in, charging sixpence for the kids and a shilling for the grown-ups, but he didn't make the money I'd been making. Still, he had to have it for himself; he couldn't see me making it, and not him.

If I wasn't getting work from Kay Lester, it came from Cissy Williams, who also used to walk across the street and buy fruit from the barrow. She was the number one boss for Moss Empires and Stoll Theatres, and her office at Cranbourn Mansions, by Leicester Square station, was right over the London Hippodrome, which later became the Talk of the Town, just across the road from my barrows in Bear Street and Great Newport Street. When there was a job going, she would pop across and weigh me in; a lot of panto bookings came that way.

Cissy was a great woman, but she was tough and knew her own mind. Her decisions could make you or break you. There were two guys called Lowe and Webster, a double act, who went for an audition at the Finsbury Park Astoria, and there was Cissy sitting in the stalls in this empty theatre, wearing this mouldy old fur coat which she wore all the year round, winter or summer, with her old spaniel dog sitting by her side. On they came and did their act. 'Rubbish,' she said, and off they went. That was all she ever said. She would never say, 'Don't phone me, I'll phone you.' She either liked you or you were 'Rubbish,' in which case that was the end of you on the Moss Empires circuit.

However, she always had a soft spot for me, and I used to take her old dog, a golden spaniel, for walks around the West End. A lovely old thing it was, with long floppy ears, and she'd say, 'Jimmy, do you want to do a pantomime? We want you for Finsbury Park, or Aston Hippodrome,' or wherever it was, and she'd always make sure that I had what we used to call the Esher Standard Contract from Equity to make sure that I got the bread.

I must have done thirty or forty pantos over the years, and it's hard to remember which was which, because the tricks were the same every year. I'd play Bonzo the Dog, or one of the Robbers, and then I'd usually have what we call a 'front-cloth routine', where I'd step in front of the main curtain while the stage hands were changing the scenery, and give the audience a bit of patter.

> I'm just a small little guy. How are you all? I shouldn't be a dwarf. I should be 6ft tall, but I'm going to tell you something. There are a lot of you people here tonight, lucky boys and lucky girls (laughter). Now, when I was a little boy (another laugh). I apologise. I'm still a little boy now (laughter), and I will tell you a story . . . all I have to say is that I am so happy to be on this land because when I see you all I am feeling very grand. Now you have paid your money to come and see the show, but you didn't come to see me, so now I've got to go . . .

It may sound a bit naff but it keeps the show moving, and that's what you have to do in pantomime.

I was in pantomime one year with Billy Reid, who was Dorothy Squires' first husband. He was a darling. Then I also did two pantomimes down at Swansea. Stan Stennett and I were playing the robbers in *Babes in the Wood* at the Grand Theatre with Ossie Morris and Maudie Edwards, while Harry Secombe was playing at the Empire. Our show ran for sixteen weeks, and I saw a lot of Harry Secombe out on the golf course.

Ossie Morris could have had a good career. He had been a coal-miner, had a good voice, and this one great song, *If I Was a Blackbird*, in the days when a good number like that was like a trademark. Everyone knew that song and they went to the theatre waiting to hear him sing it, but Ossie was a bit simple for our business, and very crude. One night I gave him a dig. Now I can be crude if I want to be but he was crude all the time, and we were standing in the wings waiting to go on when he said something way out of order, so I whacked him one, and he fell across a radiator cutting his hand. There was a bit of claret, but I still had to go on and do my next routine, but it was on my mind that he had another one coming. As we come off stage, Stan Stennett says, 'Leave it . . .'

'What's gotta be done has gotta be done,' I told him, and gave Ossie a hiding in the toilets. The trouble was he thought he was a star but he didn't last five minutes; I told him he'd be better off going back down the pit.

I had a good time down in Swansea; met a couple of nice girls. One was called Dorothy, and her brother was a butcher; he took me to the slaughterhouse one day to show me how he cut up pigs, sheep and cattle because I'm always keen to learn something new. I've always liked Welsh girls; they're the sexiest in Britain, and when they like you, they really love you, and give you everything they've got, or at least that's been my experience and I've worked all over Wales.

After we'd done that pantomime together Stan Stennett and I started a double act, with me as his stooge. We didn't work together every week but when we had bookings we went all over the country, working the variety theatres and the whole of the Moss Empires and Stoll Theatres circuit. I worked with him for about four years but I was always doing other things in between.

One year, Cissy booked me into a pantomime at Finsbury Park Empire where Yvonne Marsh was the principal boy. She had a nice voice, a lovely girl, and I tried to chat her up but couldn't get on the firm. 'You're too small for me,' she said. 'Let's go to bed,' I told her 'and then you'll find that we're the same size,' but she wouldn't have it.

With Cissy and Kay Lester looking after me, I was seldom short of work, and would still turn my hand to a bit of villainy when the right bit of information came along, 'cos I'd be down the Soho clubs every night once I'd finished a show in the London area.

One day this woman [deleted], a niece of Lord X [name deleted], gave me some information about a gaff in

Kensington, down Holland Park Road. She was not crooked, but she knew I was, and I was trying to get my leg over. I was involved with someone else at the time, but you know how it is. I like my women. Anyway, she's a good-looking bird, tall and slim, and gives me this address, and I goes over there with the twirls and lets myself into the flat.

As soon as I look into the room, I says to myself, 'This must be a recluse or a wrong 'un', because there was clothes and garbage everywhere, and on the dressing table there was an envelope. I looked inside and there was money in it and a rent book. She was obviously poorer than I was and an old-age pensioner, so I put it back on the table and slipped in another fiver, 'With the Compliments of Little Legs', because Christmas was coming up and I've never been into hurting old ladies and people worse off than me. Never rob the poor, my father said – and I don't!

Another night I was down in East Ham, by the station, and I saw this jeweller's window. I could see from the way he had wired his burglar alarm that if I smashed through a small pane in the corner, I could put my hand in and reach a nice little groin, without triggering off the alarm, so I popped that in the bin and went home. Next morning I goes down to the Grave Maurice, to see Uncle Charlie, who was the Krays' uncle on their mother's side. There were three Charles in the family – their Dad, their brother, and Uncle Charlie who was one of the best fences in the East End of London. There was another great fence called Bogie Tibbs. We called him Bogie because he was always ducking and diving, and he was one of the Tibbs family who had another big firm going. There were several other fences, too, and I had one who had a big jeweller's shop, and he used to help me shift the bigger stuff. We were well organised with plenty of fixers, bent solicitors and accountants who would sort things out for you when you had something big. Nine times out of ten, they were good Yiddisher boys who knew their way around.

No matter where I was working, I kept going back to the East End because the Kray Twins made me welcome. Their mother, Violet, thought the world of me and I thought the world of her. I had known them all for years. We're the same blood, years back; part-gypsy, part-Jewish, part mid-European, and I'd known them since before they went into the army. I don't know why they liked me so much but they were all very good to me, the whole family. Violet and their old man, and their uncles Charlie, Alf and Joey, their aunts and their grandparents – all of them made me welcome in their homes, invited me to eat with them. They were good people, with no racial prejudices, and you'll never hear me say anything bad against them because they always looked after their own.

That was the great thing about Reggie and Ronnie, they treated me as if I was the same as anyone else. It was like being part of a family. If I was in trouble and wasn't about, they would always phone up to find out where I was and what was the matter. They used to worry about me, and not just me; they looked after all of us when we were on the firm. If we were in trouble with the Old Bill, they would bring in a firm of solicitors to help us. Those boys may have done wrong but, honest to God, they never done anything to hurt an innocent person.

Uncle Charlie was one of the best. He used to live further up Vallance Road, going towards Bethnal Green. He was a big feller and always had a smile on his face. I used to go round to his flat to do the business, or meet him down at the Grave Maurice. His door was always open, and the first thing he'd always say was, 'What you got on?' and I'd say, 'Nothing.' Then he'd say, 'What d'you want?' and I'd say, 'Give us a cock and hen', and then once he'd given me the tenner, I'd say, 'What do you think of that?' and show him whatever I had in my pocket.

He would always give me something to drink because

he always had plenty of whisky, brandy, gin and whatever in the house, and then he'd leave me there while he went into his own little room, weighing it if it was gold, or checking the hallmarks. 'All right' he'd say. 'What sort of dough are we talking about?' because I always trusted him. He never, ever let us down. He was the number one, and he handled a lot of the stuff that came through the firm, and for a lot of other firms as well, but you'd never think it to look at him because he never dressed up, always wore the same old clothes, with an open neck shirt and scarf. The only times he ever dressed up was at weekends or when he had to meet the Mafia. He handled grands, but not too big. He didn't handle the Great Train Robbers' money, though he got rid of a few quid for them. He was good at laundering, and he kept things separate from the twins when it was wise. All that money they made through long firm frauds was laundered by a guy down Forest Gate [name deleted], who was also related to them.

When I took that ring in to the Grave Maurice his answer was typical. I always took my time, wouldn't ask where he was, would wait until he came in, and then wait until he had had time to have his first drink before asking if we could have a little talk, and then we'd go to the toilet because it was always the rule; we never did business in the bar. 'It's only nine carat,' he says, which I knew, 'but the stone's a sunbeam ... and I'll give you a long 'un for it.' Now he said he was taking a chance because the gold was poor, but he gave me the money there and then, and when I saw him again that evening he said it had been OK. 'Are you happy?' he says.

'Too right,' I says, because I was always pleased to have a bit more cash in the bin.

'Well, that's all right then,' he says, because that's the thing when you do a deal with a fence. Never be greedy. If he's happy and you're happy, you've both had something out of it.

The firm still kept meeting at the Grave Maurice, right through the fifties and into the sixties, long after the twins started opening their own clubs. The first club they had was the Double R, the one that Reggie opened while Ronnie was banged up; that was close to the Bow Road tube station, just by the entrance to the post office depot. Reggie chose all the decorations, fitting it out with fancy wallpaper and velvet curtains, with a specially made sign over the door linking their initials together like the logo for Rolls-Royce. It became *the* club to go to at the weekends, the first club down East that looked like a West End club, and Reggie (and later Ronnie) would be there on the door, dressed in a dinner or a smoking jacket, welcoming the actors, writers and artistes who started coming down with their wives and girlfriends.

It was a good club. There was never any trouble, and if I hadn't been around for a day or two a phone call would come through saying that Reggie had left me a message down at the Double R. That would be the sign that they had been missing me, and I'd know that as soon as I walked in the bar, Alan, the barman, would hand me the envelope in which there would always be a long 'un (£100). The boys always did that, because they'd think that you might not have come down to the Grave Maurice because you didn't have much bread, and they'd never like you to join them without being able to stand your round. They were very thoughtful; never wanted their friends to be embarrassed and never gave them money in front of anyone else. These long 'uns were what they called the 'entrance fee', and then I'd have a wee dram with Alan, jump in the motor, and go down to the Grave Maurice where we'd have our first few drinks of the day. We'd have a little bunny about this and that, jobs that had to be done, and so on, and then before moving on they'd always say, 'Now, are you sure you're all right?' Then I'd go across the road to the London Hospital and up to the fourth floor where I always used their loo and did a little bit of business with a couple of the porters, with whom I used to have something going, and then I'd take my time, jump back in the motor and drive up to town.

Whatever I said, it seemed to make 'em laugh, and then once I'd started we'd be talking and drinking, and were happy. We had good times. Every day was party-time because the money was rolling in (and I'm not telling you where it all came from), and four or five days a week I'd be down there with a lot of business going on. Every morning people would come down to the Grave Maurice with information which they paid well for, and then they'd say, 'This job sounds just right for you, Little Legs . . .', or for someone else, because they didn't go out on jobs themselves, blags and all that. They were the guvnors. The East End belonged to them.

Most of the work that I was doing in show business left me with plenty of time to go down to the Grave Maurice in the mornings, move around the East End and the West End in the afternoon, and then back down there in the Soho drinking clubs late evening, because many of the bookings were in the London area. I did three seasons in pantomime at the London Palladium, and three long ice shows at the Wembley Empire Pool – *Holiday on Ice* with Sonja Henie, *Snow White and the Seven Dwarfs* with Jacqueline Du Bief, and *Sleeping Beauty*. In those shows I used to have a comedy routine to do, like jumping over a row of beer barrels and then falling on my bum, and once I'd done those two or three-minute routines I'd be free for the rest of the day, unless there was a matinée.

Snow White and the Seven Dwarfs was one of the most successful shows I did. Before taking that on, I toured with the Morton Fraser Harmonica Gang for nine months, but that didn't work out too well and I ended up having a bust-up with Morton, so I was glad of the Wembley run. It meant I was close to home. I spent sixteen months with that show. We did that first season at the Wembley Empire Pool and then went on tour, taking in Glasgow, Bristol, Newcastle, Birmingham, Manchester and Liverpool, before appearing in summer season at Brighton and then returning to Wembley for another Christmas show.

There was a special Royal Command Performance of the show in Liverpool, attended by the Queen and Prince Philip. Gerald Palmer, God rest his soul – he liked a drink – made all the arrangements. We all had to wear our masks, standing in a row on a red velvet carpet in the foyer for the presentations to the royal couple, and we had only twenty minutes between the first show and the next. Now, I had this mask on and there are two things that make me sweat; wearing a mask and being on ice. Makes you sweat like a pig. The Queen had her white gloves on and when she came up to meet me, I gave a bow and said nothing. 'Nice to meet you,' she says, and moves on. The Prince comes next and says, 'You must be hot in there!' I says, 'To be honest, I've just had a shower and haven't had time to dry myself!' But he wouldn't have known that I was being sarcastic.

During the first season at Wembley, I'd been going out with this dancer called Pat Stringer. She was a nice girl and she'd found herself a flat just across the road from the Empire Pool, which was handy, but I hadn't told her that I'd been booked for Glasgow as well and we'd said our good-byes.

Anyway, we arrived in Sauchiehall Street, and I went into this bar which is called The Dorchester now. It's still there, but then it was called Allen's Hotel because it was owned by this geezer Allen McGregor who always wore plus-fours. I had been there before when I'd been touring in variety, so straightaway it's a wee dram, and I says to him that if anyone comes looking for me he's to tell them that I'm not there. Anyway, I goes up to my room, has a shower and changes, thinking about the rehearsals we have the following morning, and comes back down to the bar. Allen says to me, 'Are you happy?'

'Yeah,' I says. 'Sweet as a nut!' and I'm standing there, talking to a man called Pickard, an old guy from Hull, who was said to be a millionaire, although he wasn't much taller than me.

All of a sudden I hears this voice ringing out across the bar. 'You lying little bleeder,' she shrieks, and it's Pat Stringer.

'Hello,' I says, trying to keep my cool and be polite.

'You lied to me,' she says.

'It was only a white lie.'

'Do you want to stay with me, or don't you?' she says, standing there in front of everyone in this bar.

'No,' I said. 'It's all over. It was nice when it was nice, but it's all over, pet.' Then I got her and the girl that she was with a drink, and said, 'Now, do yourself a favour, pet. Leave me alone. You've been good to me. I've been good to you. We were happy, but the love stakes are not on. I have got to be free,' and I goes upstairs to my room, and leaves them in the bar. Later Allen McGregor comes up the stairs and knocks on my door. 'Are you all right in there?' he says. 'Are you comfy? Do you need a drink?' and I says to him that I have got to move out, and he gives me the address of a theatrical boarding house, where I think I'll be able to stay without being bothered by Pat Stringer.

I goes to this address the following morning, and a woman comes to the door. She's in her thirties, and I asks her, 'Do you have any vacancies?'

'Are you a professional?' she says, and I tell her that I am appearing at the old Glasgow Empire (we were the last show to appear there before it closed down).

'Normally, I only take workers,' she says. 'Builders, and so on . . .' Well, I am only in the house an hour and she's offering me coffee, and then she's bringing out the Scotch before showing me to my room. 'I do suppers and all,' she says, and I tells her not to bother because I work late, but that I do like vegetables, if there are any left over. Well, I comes back late at night, and there she is; I asks if I can have a shower, and she shows me to her bathroom. 'That's nice. I can do ten lengths,' I tell her, as she starts running the bath water, and then I'm lying down, having a nice soak, when she comes back with a warm towel.

Well, I can see what's coming, can't I? 'Can you just wash my back?' I says to her. Then while she's doing that she says. 'You're cute,' and I know that whenever they say that everything is going to be all right, and the she wraps the towel around me, takes me into her room, rubbing me dry like a little baby, and it's obvious I'm liking it.

'Is there anything else you'd like?' she says.

'Well, first,' I told her, 'I'd like a wee dram!'

Chapter 6

During those sixteen months with *Snow White and the Seven Dwarfs*, I pulled five of the girls in the show. I had no chance with some of them, 'cos there's a lot of lesbians in ice skating. Still, there was no way I had to go home at night. We'd go off afterwards, make love, and then I'd drive off down to Soho to see the boys, because that's the great thing about club life. It goes on all night, if you want it to.

When the show hit Brighton, there was another girl I fancied. Her name was Patricia Lendrum. She was 5ft 10in. and gave me the knock-back.

And then many months later, maybe a year, I'm working my fruit barrow down Argyll Street when, all of a sudden, who should walk out of the subway to Oxford Circus tube station? Long Legs.

'Nice to see you,' she says.

'Gor blimey,' I said. 'Long time, ennit? How are you, pet? Where are you working?'

'I never thought I'd see you again,' she says.

'Well, here I am,' I says, blah, blah, blah, and then asks her if she'd like to go for a drink.

'No, I've gotta go to work,' she says, and by then she was working as a hostess down at the Latin Quarter in Wardour Street. A horrible job. Very hard work. You have to sit there all night being nice to these wallies who've got money in their pockets and want a bit of sex. It's all a hustle, because the girls have to get them to spend their money on champagne – and then there's no nookie at the end of it.

So later that night I goes down to see her at the Latin Quarter, and she comes over to the table to have a drink with me. She was a tall, slim, good-looking girl, pretty with dark hair, a bit similar to Joan Collins. 'What time do you finish?' I asks her, and she says about a quarter-to-one, and I tells her that then I'll be down at the club, which was a Maltese drinking club in Archer Street, near where Charlie Chester's is now.

Every time I bump into a woman, it's always infatuation, not love. They think I'm cute and they like my 'gor blimey' accent. I lived with Heddy Horden as a common law wife for three or four years, and I've been married twice since. Even Patricia turned round and said to me, 'You don't love me.'

'What's love, baby?' I said. 'You tell me what love is . . .' and they can't. I can't explain what love is. I love flowers, but the only time I have ever told a woman that I love her has been when we've been in bed. 'I think the world of you,' I tell 'em, and then next morning it's 'Geddup!' – especially if they're gonna make me a cup of coffee or a cup of tea.

That girl who followed me to Glasgow, Pat Stringer, said, 'You don't love me,' and when I said, 'What are you talking about? What's all this about love?' she smacked me over the head with her handbag. I don't believe in love, although I can say that I love my children.

Anyway, that night Patricia comes down to the club and we took a minicab down to her flat which was about a mile from Clapham Common. What I liked about her was that she was very, very particular. 'You're not going to touch me until you've had a swim,' she says, and I'll never forget that because there was no hot water. It was winter, and it was cold putting my arse in the water. By the time I got back to bed, Trish was stripped off. 'You'd better keep on loving it,' I told her,' because it's gotta get warm. That bleeding water's frozen. I'd better buy you a bleeding kettle.'

That night ended up with me getting involved, and then we lived together down in Clapham for a year or more before we got married. She had been born in Wales, but then she had been adopted by this dentist and his wife who couldn't have children. They lived down in Sussex, near Brighton, and had brought her up with another child that they'd also adopted. I couldn't stand her 'mother' who was what we call a crafty drinker. She used to have a drink but hide the glass behind the curtains.

We didn't tell either of our families that we were getting married until the day we went to the register office at Caxton Hall, and then she phones her mother up and says: 'I'm married.'

'Who to?' says her mother. 'You haven't married HIM?'

Now I'm in the other room and I can hear the phone call, and Trisha saying, 'Mum! He's as good as gold, and, anyway, I love him!' That night we had a party at the Kismet Club, which I'd just opened in Great Newport Street, just for those family and friends that we could get in touch with at such short notice. We'd married by special licence and hadn't had time to organise anything much.

In those days I had two girls working for me. I had met them in a pantomime at Aston Hippodrome, and when the season ended I brought them down to London and set them up in a flat. They were brasses and I was poncing. I found them the place to work and furnished it for them, all nice and tidy, and said, 'Do what you want to do – and bring me a present back' or 'Just give me an envelope.' Then I'd wait down at The Salisbury pub in St Martin's Lane, which is a queers' pub now but at that time it wasn't, and they'd do their business, come back to the pub, give me a little kiss on the cheek, and hand me the envelope. 'Everything all right, babes?' I'd say, but if ever there was any trouble they'd know where to find me to sort it out.

Soho has always been a dangerous place. There has always been sex and violence, with people disappearing without a trace, and it's still like that now. Nothing's changed, only the people who run the show. Most of the punters who came to Soho got what they came for.

Sometimes you'd get the odd one who was a bit cheeky. Then I'd have to give 'em a backhander and tell 'em to get on their bike. The girls would come down to the pub if a geezer was causing problems. You'd get these guys who were quite happy being silly until they had to pay for it. I'd sort them out. No one asked them to come.

There's a skill in poncing. You should never run too many girls at any one time because they can get jealous and some nights there'd be heavy music. They might have a punter up in their flat who was getting kinky or wouldn't weigh in with the dough, and that happened time and time again. I'd tell 'em, 'Now do yourself a favour. Weigh in, because otherwise you're not going to get outside that door!' Some nights it was harder. One of the girls came down one night and said, 'I've got a nutter.' When he saw me, he freaked out. They all did, because of my size. 'Now, git!' I told him. 'Fuck off!' and I had to do the same with the geezers who wanted to stay for an hour once they'd had their ten minutes, and those who fell asleep after they'd had what they came for. You can't have that because the girl needs the bed!

In the old days a ponce used to give his birds a slap and rule them with a bit of fear, but I've never done that. A good ponce just has to be nice and sweet, and the trick is to look after a girl so that she's a bit infatuated with you. The girls have to like your style and then they let you look after them.

A good ponce never asks for money. He never asks for anything. If the girls like you, they go to work and then when they come back they give you an envelope. That's how I've always worked, even in America when I was poncing on the circus. All you've gotta do is pull a bird, and then if they say they're naughty girls you tell 'em, 'Never mind. I still like you' or 'What's that? What's a naughty girl?' and then if they say they are on the game, you say, 'What's that?' or 'Are you playing cards?' or something, all innocent, and then they come out with it and tell you that they're prostitutes. 'Well, pet. That's your problem, but I think the world of you.'

'Do you?' they say, and they end up asking you to go back home with them to their place for a bit of scranny. Later on I'll tell 'em, 'You go and do what you've gotta do – and then I'll see you when you come back home.'

Sometimes, I'd help the girls find punters. You can see a bloke walking slowly down the street, looking for something, and you say, 'Excuse me, sir. Would you like a nice girl?' And that would be a punter. And then you've got what we call a face. That's another form of punter. A face is a mug. Any bloke who comes up to Soho on his own is asking for it; he's looking for it, especially these geezers with their bowler hats and their briefcases. 'How are you?' they say, and then they whisper, 'Can you tell me where I could find a nice girl?'

'Just give me two seconds,' I tell them, while I take a wee dram, and then it's 'Come with me' and then I'd take them up to Old Compton Street or Lisle Street. 'Have you got enough money?' Out comes the wallet. I cops mine first, and then says 'Just wait here two seconds' and then I goes indoors and see whoever I want to see. 'There's a punter downstairs. Can you cover?' Then he goes up, has his ten minutes or whatever, and once I see him come out I creep back up and collect my percentage. In them days I could get two or three quid from the punter, and then go upstairs and cop another couple of quid from the girl. That's the name of the game, isn't it? That was when I was working out on the street, but other nights I would wait down at The Salisbury pub and every night at quarter to nine the girls would come in, give me a kiss on the cheek, and pass me the envelope.

Patricia was still working at the Latin Quarter, and she knows I go down to The Salisbury but she doesn't know why. One night she has her period and doesn't feel like going to work and so she comes down to The Salisbury. I'm sitting there at the bar, having a quiet drink, and she walks in the door. I says 'Hello' and buys her a drink and then in walks this brass, Jean, who doesn't know I'm married. She gives me a kiss and hands me the envelope, not noticing Patricia. 'Do you want a drink, pet?' I says, and introduces them.

When she's finished having her drink, Jean goes and says, 'I've gotta get back to work, babes' and I know the music is coming.

'What's all this about?' says Patricia, as Jean leaves the bar. 'What's in that envelope?' I tells her that it's a message from someone in the nick, but she takes it out of my pocket and opens it. 'You're a little ponce,' she says.

'That's all right,' I says. 'Keeps you going!'

Well, now she starts thinking. Here she is, having to go in to the Latin Quarter every night, which was bloody hard work, sitting there for hours with all these gullible people, these stupid idiots who think they can get you to bed if they buy you drink, talking crap, and she says: 'You're taking a bit of a risk. They could get you for living on immoral earnings ... let me take over and I'll come down here instead.' And she did. I told the two girls and they didn't mind, and I was still hanging around to help them whenever they had a problem. Trisha wasn't a bad kid. She had never known who her real parents were and she had had a hard life. She looked after me when I was in the nick, and even went out on the streets herself when she needed the money to buy me food when I was banged up in Brixton; they used to let your family bring in a meal and a half-bottle of wine in those days, and she'd bring this in for me in a billy-can.

Trouble was, with the life she had led, she didn't want a family. She was upset when she became pregnant, and I got wild. 'Is it mine?' I said, and she told me that she hadn't been with anyone else.

'So it must be mine,' I said, and I'm talking about before the pill came out.

'I don't want it,' she says.

'You've gotta have it, babes,' I told her, because it was mine as much as hers, and, fair play to her, she did, although she had very bad nerves. I wasn't there when the baby was born. I was in France. But I wanted her to have the baby because I'd never been sure that I could make babies of my own. Twice there had been girls who had told me that they were having babies that were mine, but I'd never been sure that they were and, like most men, I wanted a child of my own.

Ever since I'd come back from America, I'd never really tried to settle down. It had always been a little bit of this and a little bit of that. I still had the fruit barrows, the girls were working, there'd be a pantomime season nearly every Christmas, but that was never enough. I still had a go at anything that came up, but now I got myself a large house down in Ilford and *almost* began to enjoy married life. I'd still go down the clubs, because if I didn't Reggie and Ronnie would phone me up at home, and then send over Ronnie's Buick to take me and Trisha up to town. They were always very thoughtful; they'd send the car and the driver, and then later, after Karen was born, a babysitter to look after her. I was still on the firm and into all sorts of villainy.

While I'd been working on my things, Reggie and Ronnie had moved up West. After the Double R Club, they'd opened another in Wellington Road, also in Bethnal Green, before moving into the Soho protection business, and then taking over a much more up-market gambling club, Esmeralda's Barn in Wilton Place, Belgravia. Clubs were the thing in those days. In 1962, I had opened a club for midgets in Gerrard Street, Soho, and then the Kismet Club in Great Newport Street, and that same year they also opened the Kentucky Club down in the East End. We saw a lot of each other, still meeting down at the Grave Maurice in the mornings, and sometimes they'd call me in as a debt collector when the gamblers hadn't paid their dues. I was still into everything.

Once I robbed this jewellers shop and got away with £14,000. Two years later, the police came for me and said: 'We know you did it.'

'Did what?'

'That jewellers.'

'What are you talking about?'

'You know, and we know you did it.'

'There are a lot of other dwarfs around like me,' I told them, because by then, through opening up my Midgets Club I knew most of the dwarfs and midgets, and it's true that there were a lot, although maybe not so many like me!

'Eleven months ago you took £570 off a gentleman in Grays in Essex,' they said.

'What are you talking about?' I said. Now, in those days I didn't have a beard like I do now so perhaps I was a little less noticeable, although that's debatable. I spun them along a bit and then said, all innocent-like, 'If I'm accused of all these things, am I entitled to have an identity parade?'

'Yes,' he says.

'Well,' I told him. 'There's a lot of little people about, you know. You go and get some of the others, and then I'll have that identity parade, as you say I'm entitled to it.'

This copper took off his hat, scratched his head, looked at me, and then looked at his mate. 'He's fucked me,' he said. 'He *has* fucked me,' and he gave me a packet of Benson and Hedges and told me that I could go.

It was another bit of villainy that got me into trouble just before Trisha and I got married. I had entered a flat in Hertford Street, Mayfair, using a twirl to get in through the door, and had picked up some gold and some nice jewellery, but the Old Bill captured me. I was spotted walking down the street, and of course, being my size I'm a dot on the card. They charged me with that and another little job that I'd done up in Stoke Newington, and I was banged up in Brixton for thirty-five days before the case came up at the London Sessions. That case caused a sensation because Patricia went into the witness box and told the Chairman, Mr R. E. Seaton, how she had met me in *Snow White and the Seven Dwarfs,* how we had fallen in love, and said that I had only done those two jobs to raise a bit of money so that we could get married. That was it: 'The Dwarf Who Fell in Love with the Showgirl.' Seaton let me off with two years' probation, and next day the story was all over the national papers. It was the front-page lead in *The Daily Mirror* and *The Sunday People* followed this up with a serialised life story, which only told the things I felt like telling at the time.

You can't imagine how many press were there that day. Hundreds. They wanted to know everything about us. It was as if I was Al Capone. They followed us across the street to the Charrington pub, right opposite the steps of the Old Bailey, and there she sat, happy as a sandboy, with her gin and bitter lemon. She had lovely long legs, and I wasn't jealous of all those reporters and photographers making eyes at her because she was mine.

To be honest, I was never a good husband and when the chance came up a few months later to go on a midget wrestling tour of France I jumped at it, and took Tommy Gallagher with me to Paris. Trisha was already expecting the baby, but this was money and I had booked her into the most expensive private maternity home in Sussex, at Hove, where we had taken a house so as to be not too far from her family's home.

Tommy was excited. 'I've never been on a plane before,' he says. He was then aged 27, and as we were slipping on our safety belts the air hostess comes round and asks him if he would like a drink. 'Do you do brown ale?' he asks her. Going to France! And then he looks up through the window at the clouds and says, 'This is high up, isn't it', and we're flying over the Channel when he tells me that he has never had his leg over.

Well, I know there's a motor waiting to pick me up and

although I've taught him how to wrestle I haven't told him what we've gotta do when we get there, and I could see that his bottle had gone on the plane. You know that boxer Charlie Magri? Well, his uncle was one of the promoters for this tour and he meets us at Orly Airport, drives us into the city and takes us to this hotel which had no bar. 'You've got a room and I've got a room,' I said to Tommy. 'We'll go upstairs, have a shower, clean ourselves up ... and then I'll take you down town to introduce you to the girls.'

To cut a long story short, Tommy gets all tidy and so do I and we go down to this hotel in the Place Pigalle, where I'd been many times before. It was the place where all the brass, the prostitutes, hung around the bar, and we're sitting there, having a vodka and orange, when Tommy whispers to me. 'Aren't they nice?'

I says, 'What?'

'Aren't they nice?' he says again, still speaking in a whisper.

'Which fucking one do you want?' I asked him. Know me; I don't care who hears me.

'Will they?' he says. TWENTY-SEVEN YEARS OF AGE, and still whispering.

'Now come on,' I says. 'Make your fucking mind up. Which one do you want? That one ...' I walks across the bar and says to this bird, 'Here, I want to talk to you. Do you want to take him for a walk?' because I can talk a little French, or as much as you need in that situation, anyway. By now Tommy's eyes have gone all glassy. Walkies! He's got it! Twenty minutes later, he comes back, eyes shining. 'Everything all right?' I asks him, and he starts whispering again. 'Yes,' he says, and then while he goes off to the loo I calls her over again.

'Here, did you give him a good time?' I asks her. Now French birds are very clean. They take it out and give it a wipe for you before you get down to business, and she said she was just cleaning him up when ... whoosh! That was the end of Tommy Gallagher's big night out! It's all over! 'And you took his money?' I said. Twenty new francs it was, in those days. So who do you think got the kiss?

We had been over in Paris for three months when the phone call came through from Trisha to say that she had just had the baby. That was in the early hours of the morning on 6 December, 1963. We'd just got back to the hotel and were having a nightcap. The promoters drove me straight to Orly Airport. It was bloody cold at that hour of the morning. There was fog at Orly, and I was given all that spiel about planes not being able to take off, but they still found me a seat, first class, in one that was just leaving for London. From Heathrow, I should have caught a train, bus or coach to Gatwick, but I couldn't hang about so I hailed a taxi and asked the driver to take me straight to Hove. He couldn't believe it, but I was so excited that I couldn't stop talking, about me and Trisha and the baby, and how I hadn't seen my wife for three months because I'd been wrestling in Paris, and by the time we got to the maternity hospital he was so moved that he said: 'I can't take any money off you.'

No one would ever believe it, but we got to the hospital within four hours of me getting the phone call in Paris. Trisha was still sleeping, so the sister showed me into a room and said, 'Your daughter's very pretty', and then she took me into this ward where there were lots of little babies, all lying in their cots. She told me that the baby had weighed 6½lb at birth, but as soon as I saw her I knew that she was going to be small like me, just by looking at the arms, the legs and the body.

When Trisha woke up I told her that I couldn't stay long, and that I had to get back to Paris to finish my business, but that I'd brought back plenty of money with me and that she'd be all right.

'What's she like?' says Trisha.

'Do you want me to tell you now, or tomorrow or the next day?'

Then the tears came, and I told her, 'She's going to be small like me.' Trisha had had a hard time, anyway. It's all right for us men stuffing them up, but they've got to do the bird, carry the weight, and change the nappies. She was upset and didn't want me to go back to Paris, so I said, 'All right. I'll stay a couple of days.' They let me sleep overnight at the maternity hospital, and then the next day I took her back to this place that we had rented in Vernon Terrace, in Hove. What happened then was that I flew back to Paris and from there to Toulouse and then to Geneva and from there to Belgium, using those as the bases for midget wrestling in different countries. It was good money, but Trisha was very lonely and I must have been gone another six months. When I came back she told me that she didn't want to bring Karen up, so I drove down to Hove in my motor, put her on the back seat and brought her back to London. Karen was then 6 months old.

'I'll take the baby,' I told her, 'but what you've gotta do if we're gonna get divorced is get it done right,' because I'm a wicked little fellow. I wanted it done right so there's no going back. 'You want to go your way, and that's all right with me. What you've gotta do is let me arrange for a solicitor to come to see you. I'm not going to be cruel to you, but he'll provide you with a bit of paper, and all you have to do is sign on there and say you've committed adultery with a man unknown, and you won't even have to appear in court.'

'Where are you taking the baby?' she says.

'Babes, if you don't want to bring her up, that's none of your business. Why should you know that?'

And that was the end of my marriage. When the case came up before the divorce court, I went to the court myself to appear in person because I wanted custody of the baby. Trisha was a good ice skater, one of the best, and that was what she wanted to get back to. She had rejected her own baby because the baby had been born a dwarf like me.

Chapter 7

One night I was working my fruit barrow in Argyll Street, and a black girl comes up to me and says she is having trouble with a poofter who won't leave her alone. People often came to me with their problems. They knew I was game, and I had met this girl and her mother before. Her name was Stella.

She tells me where to find the geezer, so I gets one of the brass weights that I used to have on the barrow and goes up to this café in Rathbone Place. I gave him one. Hit him on the chin. Knocked him out, sweet as a nut. Now once they're on the deck, they never get up, because that's when I give them the Glasgow Kiss or the Dandruff, and I done him like a kipper. He was out of the game.

All of a sudden someone touches me on the shoulder, and I turns round and gives her a slap on the face before I realise it's a policewoman. Then two coppers came up and picked me up by the arms so that my feet were right off the floor. They didn't bother to get a van. They just carried me, dangling like that, to the Tottenham Court Road police station and put me in a cell. Now, it's coming back to me. I have slapped a woman, and I don't like doing that. Even worse, it's a policewoman – and *they* don't like that!

Later that night the policewoman comes round to my cell and opens the little window. 'Pet,' I says. 'What can I say? I'm sorry. I didn't mean to do it.'

'Don't worry,' she says. 'Forget it. I'm not complaining. You're just being done for hitting the bloke.'

So next morning I'm up before the magistrates, and this poofter is there with a bandage around his head, doing a moody, feeling sorry for himself, and this girl Stella turns up in court to give evidence for me. I didn't know it but she had been round to see the Old Bill the night before and made a statement, and now she turns up in court.

As I'm standing in the dock the magistrate said: 'Do you plead guilty or not guilty?'

'Yeah, guilty.'

'Have you got anything to say?'

'Yeah. That geezer over there was taking liberties with my girlfriend while I was working, and all I had done was to protect her. I was working hard with my fruit barrow and my little lady-friend was sitting in the café waiting for me, and then that geezer came in and was very, very insulting. Plus, he's a poofter and he was jealous because he fancied me. He was importuning.'

Whoooosh! I'm out of court and he gets three months.

Stella moved in with me after that, and we lived together for many months. She was a great kid, a good friend, and I still see her around.

People often came up to me when I had the barrows. I had a reputation. Sometimes I'd go out picking up debts, or sorting out a wrong 'un. Everyone knew me, see. Soho has been my home for forty years, more or less.

Another time, this brass, Faye, came up to me. She's still working around Leicester Square, has a flat down there with a red light on the door. I think a lot of her, although I haven't had my leg over. I think of her as a friend. Sometimes I want to be alone, and this night I'm sitting on the step, having just come out of the pub.

'Royston, Royston,' she says.

'What's the matter with you?'

'There's a rat on my doorstep,' she says, and this is gospel true, and she had to leave her front door open so that the punters could get upstairs. So I goes over there with my walking stick and there it is, a bleeding great rat, just like that, sitting on the stairs. I gave it a whack with my stick to make it go walkies, and, fuck me, it comes back. And then, just at the moment, the Old Bill comes down the street, two of them, and they says, 'What's that fucking row?' – and then they look at this rat and their bottle goes.

'Take the stick and give it another whack,' they says, which I does, but it's still not dead, so then they takes the stick and they start hitting the rat, and there's a crowd gathering, watching this rat. You never know what's gonna happen in Soho.

There were some great characters in the old days. I knew Billy Hill and Jackie Comer, whom we called Jack Spot. That was in my father's day. And then there were the Sabini brothers, the Messina brothers, and Tommy Smithson. I knew them all. Tommy used to run a snooker hall and gambling club over a restaurant in Archer Street. Ronnie and Reggie went to his funeral when he was shot. They thought the world of him. He was a lovely guy, used to have a queers' club in the Haymarket, before the law changed, and that was where I met [names of famous stars deleted] and Shaky Sheila, who ran three clip-joints. Soho was always dangerous. It was dangerous in those days, when you had the Italian gangs and the Maltese; it was dangerous when the Krays were there, and it's still dangerous now with the Chinese. People still disappear off the streets.

The Chinese don't care because they know they're in charge. If someone upsets them, doesn't pay a gambling debt or gets out of order, they don't mess about. But I like the Chinese. They've got hearts of gold. If I'm down in Leicester Square, sitting on a step, looking depressed, they'll often slip me money if they think I need it. They're generous people; they'll ask you if you want something to eat, and give you food. I think the police are afraid of the Chinese. There are too many of them, for a start, and when there's trouble they take to the streets with machetes, thirty or forty of 'em at a time, and then the police come slowly; they don't know their way around like they used to in the old days. They always knew who was in charge, and where we were, even when they didn't know what was going on.

On Derby Day, we all went off to Epsom; a whole party of us, Reggie and Ronnie and all the boys. Prince Monolulu was a great mate of mine, and he'd turn up at the Derby every year, saying, 'I gotta horse, I gotta horse', in his head-dress and feathers like some Indian or African chief. And I'd be there, standing by his side with two other midgets, suited and booted, shouting, 'I've got a better horse than 'im!' Now what you do – and this is where there's the con – is you write down the names of every horse that's running in the race, and, say there's thirty runners, well you write out thirty slips of paper and that means someone has gotta get a winner, the second and the third. Now, you used to sell them at five shillings a slip, and I'll guarantee you that the winner would always come back, slip you a few quid and say, 'Thank you very much!' Monolulu thought the world of me, and it was he who taught me that trick ... and whenever you get a horse that comes home at great odds like 18–1 or 100–6, the winner's always grateful. I missed last year's Derby because I didn't get up in time, but I still go down to Epsom for the day, 'cos after I've done that trick I go down to Tattenham Corner, which is where all the Londoners come in their coaches, open their boots and lay out their picnics. How can I go wrong? They're all there, and as soon as they see me it's 'Hey, Kernel – how are you?' 'What yer doing?' 'Where you bin since last year?' and I gets my ukelele out and does a bit of busking.

After working Tattenham Corner, I usually go halfway up the hill on the Downs where there's a good pub, a Cockney pub, with the Pearly Kings and Queens and there, again, you cannot go wrong, especially when you're my size. At the end of the day, I can never remember how much I've handled, but when I get back home and unroll the paper, there's always three or four hundred quid, *always!* That's why all my family worry about me, 'cos I never put the money into my pocket or into a money belt. It always goes straight into my bag, and who'd mug me, with my reputation?

It was my father who brought me up to the West End. That was in the days when he was street bookmaking and took the premises at 4 Lisle Street. That was where he ran his office. He had the whole building, leased all four floors, but only used the front office, and I couldn't bear to see all that space going to waste. So my brain went working and I got the birds in, furnished the rooms and turned it into a knocking-shop. That's an easy game, 'cos all you have to do is wait downstairs for them to come to you. When they find a punter, a Yank or some other geezer, they come in the door, you give 'em the key, and then they go upstairs, do the business – which is usually just ten minutes for the short-timers – and then out they go, weighing you in as they leave. Sometimes the girls might want the rooms for longer if they'd got a long-shot in, but it was mostly ten-minutes-a-time. Good business that. No trouble with tenants, rent books and all that caper – and from the girls' point of view, they only had to pay when they had a punter. Everybody's happy! They used to call me the Midget Ponce. Time and time again.

There was a lot of money coming into Soho in those days. I'm talking about the fifties and the sixties, and I mean a lot of money. Hundreds of punters arriving every night, looking for women, booze or a little excitement, but it's all changed now. It all went too heavy, and then the Old Bill moved in, closing down the strip clubs, the bars and the clip joints, and I don't blame 'em. It had gone a bit too far. Girls were getting killed and the villains were fighting among themselves, but they were never innocent people getting hurt. That's what the press and the politicians never understood. The old timers, the Greeks and the Italians, who ran the restaurants, shops and cafés were mostly left alone. The birds and the villains got on with their business, and the customers got what they came for; the only time you had trouble was when the villains fell out or you had a kinky punter.

They all thought the world of me, especially Attilio Messina, who was very tall. He was the one that got deported home to Malta. He used to tell me, 'One day you'll be bigger than the Mafia!' Me! And I'd say, 'Maybe!' He was always immaculate, and couldn't understand how I had learned Italian, but I've been there – I've been to Naples, Rome and Milan. That was after my second tour of America.

What they liked about me was that I was always game for anything, and never lost me bottle. They could give me a job to do and there'd never be any come-back. It's what my Dad used to say, 'if you can't do your time don't do your crime'. I could do me bird, and although I ended up with twenty-two convictions – three for stabbing and two for using a shooter – and was sent down for a seven, a four, a three, a two and an eighteen months, they always knew I could be trusted.

A mate of mine, good as gold, used to have a tiny barrow selling cabbages, potatoes, carrots and a bit of fruit. He loved oysters, which was funny because he only had one eye. He was a bloody good mate, anyway, and we were going into the Britannia pub in Leytonstone High Road one night when he says to me, 'There was a bit of aggro down the road last night.'

'What was he like?'

'A bit big for you,' he says, which is what they all say, because they're all bigger than me, aren't they?

'Never mind,' I said. 'I'll sort this punk out,' which is what I call 'em – punks. 'Hang about.' So I goes down to this other pub, buys a wee dram, and clocks this big coloured guy when he goes out to the loo, and that's where I go, too, 'cos it's always the place to catch 'em.

'Now you are a twenty-two carat cunt,' I told him, grabbing him by the lapels of his coat, and telling him that he had upset my mate the night before. 'Now do you know what I am going to do to you?' Now, I'll be honest. I have got power in my muscles, or I did have in those days.

'I didn't mean it,' he says.

'Oh yeah? You didn't mean it! Now, I want to give you a little present,' I said. 'Let's shake hands,' and I've got this blade in my hand, a Stanley blade, between my fingers, and he's bleeding and I'd only done his hand; so then I gave him another one. Now, I hate cutting people's faces for the simple reason that it can take their living away. I don't mind stabbing them in the belly, or cutting them across the arms or up the bum, because that hurts but it never kills 'em, but if you do the face that leaves a scar that everyone else can see. They can go out and be Jack the Lad, but they'll never be guvnor because the one that's guvnor is the one that gave 'em the scar.

In Soho the rule was simple. You had to hold your own. If anyone ever slapped me, there had to be a come-back, whether it came that day, the next day, or the day after that. I didn't mess about.

There was a café called Theo's in Wardour Street, and they had a room downstairs with a pool table and table tennis. This guy Johnny [full name deleted] reckoned I was chatting up one of his birds, a prostitute, and slapped me across the face with a table tennis bat. Now that bloody hurts and I was bleeding, but I swallowed it. I had a Zodiac at the time, and next day I picked up my mate Nipper Thompson, told him we had to take care of someone, and asked if he was game, which he was. Nipper was a good boy. So I told him that we would go up the Edgware Road where Johnny had a fruit barrow and a flower stall and said to Nipper, 'Now what you've gotta do is go across the road as if he knows you, pull out a roll of notes, and say you've gotta weigh him in ... and he'll cross the road to see you, 'cos he's a greedy bugger.'

I was waiting just down the road in the Zodiac. Nipper calls out, 'Johnny ... I want to give you some money.' Johnny crosses the road, and I hit him right in the fucking air. I'll be honest with you. I wanted to kill him. He was in a bad way, but he never died. These days he uses a bar down near Victoria Station and every time he sees me he salutes me. He knows that he can't win, but I'll say one thing for him; he never grassed. They know that if they grass, there will always be a come-back.

There was one geezer who did grass me up, and that was when I was with the Krays. The information came back to me, and I told one of the firm to go and find him, and tell him that I had forgiven him. They found him and brought him back to me. I said, 'Now, pet. Come on. I want to take you for a drink . . .'

He said, 'Can I . . .'

'Don't. No apologies.'

There were two other lads in the motor, and I told him that we would go down to the George on Wanstead Flats. I said to him, 'You drive,' and as we're going along the road in the motor I told him, 'Now I don't want to talk about what you've done. You've done me naughty, but I've forgiven you . . . we'll have a good drink in this pub, and then we'll go to another pub.' Well, I'm ready for him, aren't I? I tell him to stop the car for a minute while I have a piss, and then we all get out and I wind up the windows and take the car key. Then I get a rope and loop it through the door handles and tie it round the car, tight, and he's still there, sitting in the driving seat, and it's happening so fast he can't take it in. Then I open the boot of the car and take out a petrol can which is full of water, although he doesn't know that, and then sprinkle it over the bonnet and the roof of the car, and he's still inside, scratching at the windows now, starting to panic and shitting himself. He's screaming, and I say, 'Bye bye baby,' and he's crying, going mental, and I gets out a box of matches, says 'Bye bye baby' again, lights a fag, and walks away. Talk about diarrhoea! I has me fag, and then comes back, takes out me tool and slashes the ropes. He's whimpering inside, covered in shit, and I says to him,

'Now before you change your pants, clean the car – and the next time it will be for real. You understand that? FOR REAL!'

It's so easy when you know how to handle them. I'm a nice little man, really, but once they turn me over – which they think they can do because I'm little – then they have to see what I can do. That's happened to me time and time again. The only people who have ever really treated me properly are my own kind, people like me, villains, like the Krays; villains and show business people are the only ones who know how to behave.

Another time, and this is still in the sixties, I opened this club for dwarfs in Gerrard Street. Tony Mulla, who was a big villain in those days, had two clip-joints down the street. He thought I was taking away his business. He was angry and was walking up and down the street, just across from my club, shouting at me, 'You think you're Jack the Lad', 'Midget Mafia,' and so on, trying to tell me that I was being cheeky and was out of order in opening my club on his patch. He was a well-built feller, Tony Mulla, and not long after he got shot in the head one day, brown bread. Anyway, I wasn't having that and took him up the stairs above his clip-joint, and, with two mates holding him by the arms, took his trousers down, and slashed him across the arse with a razor; gave him noughts and crosses.

There were no milk bottle petrol bombs in those days. If you had a problem you had to sort it out yourself. I used to carry a shooter all the time in the sixties. That was a habit I got into when I was in the States. There you could walk into stores right the way across America and buy a gun if you wanted one, and I always had a shooter after that. The thing with a shooter is that you don't have to use it. If you go out on a job, all you have to do is show it – and they start running. Believe me, they run. Sometimes I had to use it, and I'll admit that.

When I went out on a job for the Krays, they always

provided the motor, the driver and the gun, so there was no need to use your own. That way there was no comeback, because it was all taken away afterwards. On that sort of job you always had to burn your clothes afterwards just in case you were captured, so that there would be no forensic. If you had to use a shooter, you lost it – and you always wore gloves, not rubber ones but plastic, because then the Old Bill could never get fingerprints. And you always used a stolen motor, and then dumped it with the windows left open so that the early morning condensation would remove any trace of fingerprints. There again, we didn't take chances; we'd always give the steering wheel, the gear stick and the handles a wipe-down as well, because they're the only parts of a bent motor that are touched by hand when you're out on a job.

Other firms in different parts of the country would come to Ronnie and Reggie when they needed a bit of help to sort out their problems, because it's always better to send someone in from outside, someone who is not known, and I'll always say this for Ronnie and Reggie: they were always fair. They always checked to make sure that a contract was justified. No one was ever sent to do a job until they had made sure that the bloke had done what it was said he had done. I did one job for them down in Ilford where two bookmakers [names deleted] had welshed on a bet, which was naughty. They gave me jobs like that because they knew I could handle them, and they never ever sent me out on a wrong 'un.

I did other jobs for them in Birmingham, Newcastle, Manchester, Bristol and Glasgow, as well as all the other things I did in London, but I've gotta be careful how I talk about those things, even now. Yes, I have killed people, but I am not going to tell you who, where or when. None of them were innocent. They were all villains.

They sent me up to Glasgow when Johnny Stack asked for a bit of help. He was the biggest villain in Glasgow in those days, but this was a job where he thought it would be better for someone to go in from outside. Johnny's dead now so I can mention his name. He was having trouble with a bookmaker in Hamilton who was ripping off the old ladies; he was taking the money and not paying out, which is something we just don't tolerate. So I went up there by train with two other guys, and first we smashed up his windows, then we broke up his premises, before working him over with baseball bats. We didn't kill him; that was enough, but I was silly. Instead of catching the next train back to London, which I should have done, I spent a few days in Glasgow, meeting old friends and having a wee dram. The Old Bill picked me up and chucked me into Barlinnie, but they had to let me go. They didn't have the evidence.

To hear me talk, it sounds like I was into violence all the time, but we'd often go weeks without any trouble. Most of the time I was either running my club, the Kismet Club, which lasted longer than the club for dwarfs or midgets; doing these show business jobs that came in every now and then; working my barrows; helping the Krays with their protection business, and doing freelance jobs of my own. You see, the thing is I was into everything.

When I opened that club in Great Newport Street, the Kismet Club, I had to do it in my brother Raymond's name because the Old Bill complained to the licensing magistrates that I wasn't a fit and proper person to hold a licence. There was a lot of concern about clubs in those days and their links with crime. Questions had been asked in Parliament, and word was getting round that there were new gangs now operating in Soho, working the protection rackets.

Asking for protection money is so easy. I've done it many times, working for the Krays. There was nothing new about their methods. There was protection in the States when I was there; protection down the East

End before the Krays moved up West, and there was protection in Soho when my Dad was alive.

When you're setting up the owner of a pub or a club to pay protection, you walk in one evening with a few quid in your pocket, have a few drinks, buy one for the guvnor. 'Busy pub?' you say. 'Doing well?' 'Do you get any trouble here?' And then if he says something like 'Only at the weekends', you say to him, 'You shouldn't have to put up with that. We've all got a living to make. You leave it to me and my mates. We'll take care of that for you.'

'Will you?' he says, telling you that Friday is his busy night.

Now little does he know, but we send someone in to cause some trouble next Friday, to have a bit of a fight, smash up the glasses, throw a few chairs around, smash the optics, and then you let him see you sort it all out and throw the geezer out. And that's when you give him what we call 'the plug'. That's when you tell him that he will have no more trouble if he'll just let us have a bit of money for the boys, to buy them a drink. 'You look after us, and we'll see you have no more trouble,' you say.

That's how you start off and if he bites, you've got him. If he doesn't bite, then you start to get a bit more heavy. There's more violence the next Friday, and in the end he will bite. They all do. Remember, there were no private security firms in those days, no bouncers – when we provided protection, we did stop the violence, but they had to have it. Then we would go there once a week, usually on a Sunday morning after they've made all their dough for the week, and pick up the bread.

Now when my brother Raymond opened up the Kismet Club for me, we had no trouble at all. Who would ask *me* to pay protection?

Raymond was a lovely boy, tall, polite and so innocent. He had gone to the Italia Conti drama school with a little fellow called Johnny Briggs, who came from Bermondsey, and is now in *Coronation Street*. They used to come and see me when I had the fruit barrow in Argyll Street and needed the money to go off on a bender. They were good-looking boys. Raymond taught me everything he knew. In those days, the Italia Conti School was in Archer Street and Diana Dors was there as well, just a young kid; I went down there to see my Raymond one day, and found him giving her one in the phone box, up the stairs. God rest his soul! I was jealous, I can tell you, because I've never been able to do it standing up, being my size; I've always had to lay 'em on a mattress.

No one could have been better to front the Kismet Club for me because we'd opened it up for the actors, writers, agents and people in the film industry and the music business. Richard Burton used to come down there some nights, and so did Susan Shaw who topped herself after her husband Bonar Colleano was killed in a car crash; she was always bouncing cheques. Being in the business myself, I wanted to get everyone down there. Max Bygraves came down a few times but he would never spend a penny. Very tight, he was. Among the others who came down to the club were Frankie Vaughan, Arthur Haynes, Adam Faith, Yvonne Marsh, Petula Clark, and many more, because it was always a well-run, decent club, where people could have a drink and relax.

One day I was out on the street and three geezers arrived. My brother called me into the cloakroom and whispered 'It's on us,' meaning they had come down looking for us to pay them protection, and I'd never seen them before in my life.

'Just stay cool,' I told him. 'Stay behind the ramp,' and I jumped up on the bar so I had one of them standing one side of me, and the other two on the other. I says to my brother, 'Give us a large Scotch and pass the soda,' and he couldn't understand what I was going to do, because he knew I drank my whisky neat, but I wanted the syphon and I was watching the one who was standing on his own. I smashed him across the side of the head with the syphon, and as I'm doing it one of the other geezers stuck me up the bum with a blade. Well, he didn't get up the stairs. Now, at the time I had the Zodiac and I drove straight off to Paddington, to the hospital in Praed Street, so they could stitch me, 'cos my bum was bleeding bad.

'We've got to call the police,' says the doctor, and while they're doing me, putting in fifteen stitches, the Old Bill arrived.

'What happened?' they said.

'We were larking about,' I says, telling them that I had been cutting some French bread and cheese, and had left the knife on the settee and sat on it.

'Yeah, we've heard that story before.'

'Well, that's the story you're getting,' I said, and after the doctor had stitched me up and given me the dressings, they let me go. I got back in the motor and went back to the Kismet. 'Where's my Raymond?' I said when I got there.

'He's in hospital,' they said, and told me that soon after I had driven away to Paddington those geezers had come back and done him over with hammers. Raymond was taken to Charing Cross Hospital, and then he developed a tumour and I got him into the Royal Marsden, and he was paralysed. 'We've gotta do something,' I told him, and I went after the one geezer when I was given the information where he lived. That was down to the Krays. They knew where he came from, and he was what we call bad medicine. He had been into a lot of other things as well, and he had it coming to him.

The best time to get anyone who does you wrong is to get up early in the morning, when they're all tired and not expecting you. He was living down in Bow, so I went round to his flat at six o'clock. Unfortunately, his two kids came to the door, so I can't do nothing 'cos I love kids. Then I sat downstairs in the motor, 'cos I know he's gotta come out. As he walks out of the door, I shouted, 'Danny, I've got a message for you!' I wanted to knee-cap him, but he turned and started to run back into the flats so I got him below the knee and blew away his calf muscles, but fair play to him, he never grassed. He would never tell me who the others were. I went looking for them but never found them, though I'd recognise them now if they walked in the door.

Raymond died soon after that. Murdered. The Old Bill never got the blokes who did it, and I don't suppose they tried too hard. Unfortunately, my brother Raymond wasn't a violent man. If he had been up to some of the tricks that I've done, he could have survived, but I still put the blame on myself for going off to the hospital that night and having my bum stitched. I should have stayed in the club.

Chapter 8

By the time Reggie and Ronnie took on the El Morocco in Gerrard Street, there were eighteen of us on the firm. We had had a good run. The firm had been going nearly fifteen years, since before the boys went into the army, and the Old Bill had no idea how well organised we were. We took care of ourselves.

Had the boys stayed in the East End, they would still be around today. The East End was theirs. They ran it, and there was no real need for them to move up West. But they were ambitious. The firm was a business and they wanted it to expand.

Their first move West was that club called Esmeralda's Barn, which was a high society gambling club in Wilton Place, just off Knightsbridge. It looked like every other house in the street from the outside, but inside there was a gaming room downstairs, a bar upstairs, and a restaurant on the top. The rooms were nicely furnished, and the Krays took over without the regulars knowing that there had been a change in ownership.[1]

Some very posh people used the club. Peers, politicians and rich young businessmen who didn't mind losing a few grand on the gambling tables, but they didn't have to gamble if they didn't want to. The restaurant was good. People would come down in the evenings for a meal there, if that was all they wanted, and there was usually music, a trio or someone playing guitar. Princess Margaret came down. I suppose I met her three or four times. The Duke of Kent used it occasionally, too, and there were often show business people down there in the evenings. Rach-

[1] The circumstances in which the Krays acquired Esmeralda's Barn through their connection with Rachman are well described in Pearson's book *The Profession of Violence*.

man came down sometimes, and so did Christine Keeler and Mandy Rice-Davies.

Reggie and Ronnie brought me in as one of four people they had in to help them with the club. The twins thought the world of me. Whenever there was a difficult job to be done, Ronnie would say, 'Give it to Little Legs. He doesn't care whether he gets nicked or not,' which was true. I was game, and I still don't. They knew I would do the business and never talk, and that it was always business before pleasure 'cos I've always taken the view that there's another day tomorrow. If someone hadn't paid their gambling debts, I used to give them a little talking-to and if they'd been naughty, I would show them out of the door.

I had to give one famous star [name deleted] a slap for being cheeky, and then gave him another slap some time later when we heard that his wife had put her head in a gas oven. She was a good kid and we knew that he'd been way out of order.

When the members came to settle up at the end of an evening, we always liked readies. No cheques. They bounced like tennis balls. There were no credit cards in those days, but if someone went over the top we'd take a cheque and then not cash it, using it as an IOU. If they didn't come back with the cash when they said they would, I would be sent round to collect it. If they hadn't got it, then it was smacky bum-bums. When these people opened the door and saw a dwarf like me, they would freak out, but I don't think that's why the twins sent me. They trusted me because they had known my father and mother, like I knew their family. We were close.

For us, Esmeralda's Barn was a meeting place up West where we could go to do business. It started off well, making a lot of money, but then the word got round that villains had moved in. A naughty policeman dropped 'em in it with the Inland Revenue and the club didn't last three years for them.

Then we moved back down the East End again, 'cos we always had to have somewhere to meet. That was when Ronnie and Reggie opened the Kentucky Club. That didn't last long either because the Old Bill moved in and made trouble over their licence, but it was good while it lasted. The club was well fitted out with red carpets, red velvet curtains and gilt furniture, which was what people liked in those days, and there was a small stage for strippers or live music. Ronnie had me down there some nights with a donkey I had called Biba, and, just as a joke, I would ride into the bar on the back of the donkey wearing jeans, a check shirt, a scarf around my neck and a big stetson hat, with a guitar slung over my shoulder. Then I'd sit there singing cowboy songs like *Ghost Riders in the Sky* while Ronnie stood there, holding the donkey with one hand and a gin and tonic in the other. One night I was in the middle of a song, with the audience laughing their heads off, when in walked a bookie who had welshed me on a bet. I knew he must have some money on him, so I leapt off the donkey and chased 'im into the toilet. Ronnie couldn't stop laughing. Everyone else thought it was part of the joke, and they were screaming with laughter, too – but I got the money off 'im!

This wasn't an act, just a joke. I had borrowed the donkey from Billy Smart's Circus, and kept him in a field with my pony who I used to take round the pantos. That was all part of my panto act, and it went down well with the children. I used to lead Molly on stage and say to the children in the audience, 'Now my Molly is very well educated.' Then I'd turn to Molly and say, 'Have you been to school today?' and I'd dig her in the ribs without them seeing, and she'd nod her head.

And then I'd say to the children, 'Now, I want you to give me a number', and they'd all be shouting out at once, different numbers, but I'd pick say number four, give her the four digs and Molly would go nod, nod,

nod, nod, and all the children would burst out cheering and clapping.

Then I would say, 'Now, children. Do you want Molly to add or subtract? You want Molly to take five away from seven? Right,' and then she would go nod, nod, and they'd all start clapping again.

Reggie and Ronnie loved all that sort of nonsense, and they would always come to see me when I was doing shows. I appeared in three London Palladium pantomimes during the sixties, and they would come down to see every show, sometimes more than once, always dressed in their best suits with their raincoats over their arms, and often bringing their Mum and Dad, and then afterwards I would take them backstage to meet all the other artistes.

Reggie and Ronnie were bound together like superglue. When I'd first known them, all they'd been interested in was sport and they'd always made me very welcome down at their home in Vallance Road where their Mum, Violet, would always lay an extra place for me. She always had big pots of broth on the stove, and cooked lovely stews. Charlie, their eldest brother, was never really a villain. He wasn't into it, but he thought the world of the boys. Violet was a wonderful mother to them all. She was fairly short, only about 5ft 2in. or 5ft 3in., fair haired, and always smiling. She used to do a lot of charity work down the East End, helping with jumble sales and things like that, and that's where they got all that from, 'cos they always looked after women and children and the old folks.

And then when they started up their clubs, they weren't real villains. The most they might do would be to spank a few people. They weren't thieves. They had never thieved in their lives. They might have done some conning or protection, but that isn't thieving. If someone says they've got a problem and you say you'll take care of it, that's not thieving. It's protection. And the Krays did offer real protection. There were other villains wandering around Soho at the time, as well as all the Jack the Lads who might be silly in drink, and when the Krays protected a club there was never any trouble on the premises. The clubs would pay so much a week, and then the Krays would provide doormen – or bouncers, as they call them nowadays – and they'd keep all that sort of thing under control. It was more like a private security service, although those hadn't started in their day.

When you were on the firm you all stuck together. Many of us were related. We were all very close. Bless 'em, Reggie and Ronnie were true brothers, who would always stand by each other. Charlie was different. He was more selfish, always a loner. With Reggie and Ronnie, if you got into trouble the first thing they would do would be to try and get you out of it. If you got captured, they would get someone to lay on bail for you, and then they would lay you on a brief because they had two firms of solicitors working for them and they could always find you a good barrister. But they went too far in the end. There was a lot of jury-fixing going on, and a lot of money changing hands with the Old Bill before the straight coppers came along and trapped 'em. But they should never have got thirty years. I mean to say, Georgie Cornell and Jack McVitie were asking for it. They were crap.

Reggie and Ronnie never killed any innocent people. They were never into robberies or big crimes like that. They were into protection and running clubs, and through that they knew a lot of bent policemen, brasses and villains. When they got hold of good information, they would give you a whisper. That was all they did. They were done for those two murders but nothing else was ever proved against them. Their clubs brought together villains, slags and show business people. We would all go out and do our own thing during the day, and no one would know what we had done, and then we'd come back in the evening and meet at the club. The best one we ever had was the El Morocco.[2].

We still used to meet at the Grave Maurice in the mornings. Different members of the firm would drive over from Wandsworth, Clapham, Kensington and West London. We didn't all live in the East End. If there was something big on, either Reggie or Ronnie would give me a phone call and say, 'We're meeting.' They'd never say much more than that. We always took care with the telephones in case we were being tapped. Then they'd give us the information, or, if there'd been trouble, ask us to give someone a message, usually over money, though sometimes there might have been a bit of aggravation. Often I would walk in the door, rub my hands and say, 'Anything about?' and they'd always put things my way because they knew I could handle it.

Reggie and Ronnie never went out on the street themselves. They were the guvnors. But their information was always good. Some of the brasses would tell them when they'd met a punter who had money, and they'd also hear about factories and offices where there were jobs waiting to be done. I did a lot of payroll jobs, factories mostly, because they're easy, and then afterwards if they'd given you the information you'd weigh them in.

Once they told me about some kettles (watches), and they were good ones. It was a factory job and the nightwatchman was bent. All I had to do was get inside and then hand the boxes out through a window to the blokes outside. That job should have been easy, but

[2]At this point readers may find it helpful to consult the Chronology on p.209. Before opening the El Morocco, the Krays were remanded in custody to Brixton Prison, accused of demanding money with menaces from the club's previous owner. It had had another name, the Hideaway Club. Roy Smith was also in Brixton, occupying an adjoining cell, although he had been 'captured', as he would put it, for something quite separate. As they were all living their lives on so many different levels, I have brought his prison experiences together to form one section of the book, Chapter 11. Readers will have realised by now that the 'firm' still functioned, no matter who was in gaol.

things went wrong. We had agreed that I should stay inside until half past five in the morning, when the nightwatchman would come back and let me out, so I took some medicine inside with me but I couldn't rest. I kept thinking about those kettles. There must have been fifty or sixty boxes of them each containing a gross of ladies' cocktail watches, and good quality, and I was trying to think how much my share would be. By the morning I was right wanked out because I'd had no kip and was waiting to get out.

Come half past five, the nightwatchman lets me out, and I force the locks to make it look as though we've forced our way in, and go back home to clean up. The wife says to me, 'Where have you been?' and I says, 'Don't talk to me. Just let me relax and I'll tell you.'

Now, fortunately, there's drink in the house, and I have a fag and a wee dram and goes round to see the boys who'd been out on the job with me.

'Where's the gear?' I said.

'We've done it. Taken it down to the fence.'

'You're not entitled to do that. This was my job,' I said.

'You'll be happy.'

'What did it come to?'

'A monkey for you,' which is £500. When I heard that I went through the roof. All those kettles! And me being stuck in that factory for hours on end! All for a monkey!

'Hang about,' I said. 'There must have been a gross in each box, and each kettle must have been worth a wuncer.'

'We had to do it,' he says.

'You had to do sod all. I got the information. I had to go in there, hand them out through the window and then stay there all night. Now where's the fucking bread?'

I am not going to mention their names, but I knew what they had done. They had gone back to the fence, got the money and shared it out, and forgotten all about me, stuck in there on my tod, and then they'd said to themselves, 'Little Legs will be happy with a monkey.' Well, I bloody wasn't and I got a bit more in the end.

On that kind of job, you had to have help, handling so many boxes, but mostly I went out on my own. I felt better that way. Only myself to blame if anything went wrong. And I'd travel anywhere to do a job if the money was good.

There was one time I was given some information about a house in Ware, Hertfordshire, where the owner was said to have a valuable collection of jewellery and antiques. I clocked the house, and realised that the best way in would be over a flat-roofed extension and in through an upstairs window. As I climbed in through the back room window, I saw a baby lying in bed with a teddy bear. That finished me. I couldn't go on with it. I climbed straight back out of the window, and then fell off the roof, straight into a plastic dustbin. Lucky it was plastic, 'cos that made no noise. Had it been an ordinary metal bin, there'd have been a hell of a noise and I'd have been captured but this time I got clean away.

Another time I did this timber merchants down in East Grinstead, where I had been told there was a big peter. They knew I was good with plastic. I've done a good few safes, although I've never been captured for a safe-breaking. I'm very careful. All you have to do is pop the plastic in a keyhole and use a detonator. I always like to use a fuse, not electric, but when I did this job I blew out all the windows – and still didn't open the safe.

Then there was the time Reggie and Ronnie told me about this jewellers in Chelsea. The information came to me on the Monday and I goes over to have a look at it, and then I does the job at ten o'clock on the Tuesday morning. We'd been told that this woman opened the shop first, and then the manager or the owner arrived at half past ten. Sweet! On the Tuesday morning I was there by quarter past, walks in, and tells her to go into the back room. I had this buddy with me. I'm not going to mention his name. We didn't hurt her. Just told her to do as she was told, put all the tom in the bag, and then drove straight down to Uncle Charlie. I've told you about him. He was a good fence. Never pissed about. When you did a job like that, you could go straight down to Charlie. You could trust the man. He would not take a penny off you. You could give him a bag of jewellery or gold, and then go back to him later and he would tell you what your share was and he would always be fair. He was careful who he dealt with, but once he knew you and trusted you he was fair. If it was gold, he used to take a third. When it was silver, whisky, tobacco and so forth, it was fifty-fifty. That was when you were working on your own. If you had two others working with you, he would take a third, which was fair. Sometimes I might just get the one small thing that was good, maybe a groin, but I would still take it to Charlie, and then he'd get his eyeglass out, look it over, and might just take a drink out of it. He would never do me.

I was up to everything, always taking care not to do anything too big – because then the Old Bill get interested. That's where the Great Train Robbers went wrong. The job was too big. The Old Bill had to find 'em. I always liked to keep working all the time, never being greedy, and there was no trick that missed me. If someone gave me some information, I would always size the job up first, never take it too quickly, and if I didn't like the look of it, I wouldn't do it. Sometimes a message would come from a bent manager who wanted to claim insurance, or a nightwatchman, but I'd always go down and have a look first, size it up, decide whether it was a freelance job, a two-hander, a three-hander, or whatever, and what transport might be needed.

One of the greatest was down in South Benfleet before I got the land over there. I met this geezer through his daughter. This was infatuation again. Same old problem.

I got my leg over, and she said, 'Do you know what my Dad does? He drives a lorry.'

'What does he have on, pet?'

'Plenty of gear.'

It took me a long time to sort this one out, to get to know him, find out what he carried, where he went, and so on, but it was worth it because he was carrying cigarettes and you can't go wrong with cigarettes. He used to do regular runs along the M1 and I watched him, and then one day I gave him a stopper. You know what a stopper is? I drove in front of him, and made him stop, and then told him, 'I want it.' Look at the size of me! And him with a lorryload of cigarettes!

'I want it.'

That job I did on my own. There was no one with me.

'I want it,' I said again, and told him that I was going to get up in the driving cab with him and that he was going to drive his lorry down to the East End of London, 'And then you're gonna lose this lot . . .'

'I can't,' he says.

'You will.'

'How do you know about it?' he says, and then I tells him that I know who he is, where he lives, and his daughter, and that he's to do exactly as I tell him. When we get to the East End, he will park his lorry, go and have a wee-wee, and then by the time he comes back the lorry will have gone and he can phone his office and say he's been robbed.

And do you know what he had on the back that day? It wasn't bloody fags after all. It was OXO cubes! But they're good. You can always find a fence who will take a load like that and turn 'em into readies fast. The bloke was worried stiff. 'I'll get nicked,' he said.

'No you won't.'

'You know my daughter?' he says.

'Yes,' I says, and I tells him her name, where she lives, and he knows I'm on the level.

'Did my daughter tell you about this?'

'No one told me about this. I just worked it all out for myself. You just do as I tell you, and you will be all right. You just leave the lorry and then leave the rest to me.'

Next morning I drove down to see him, to give him a little present to make him happy. He nearly had a heart attack when he saw me at the door, but I said, 'Leave it out. No one knows anything. You've lost sod all . . .' And that still goes on. A lot of money is still made through stolen lorries, but you don't read about it any more 'cos the papers no longer think it's news.

Coming near Christmas-time a driver who wants to lose a load of cigarettes, cigars or spirits can always make a few quid for himself. You don't wait for them to come to you; you get into them. You find out who they are, where they live, and who they work for, and then you meet 'em, and say, 'Would you like to earn a few quid . . . all you have to do is lose your lorry.' Never bother with wine. Wine is shit. Cigarettes, whisky, maybe vodka. That's what you want. You can never go wrong with those at Christmas.

When information like that came to me from the Krays, I would go off, do the business, and then if I walked back into the Grave Maurice the next day with a smile on my face, rubbing my hands, they would know I had done OK, and then I would weigh them in. They would never, ever ask me how much I had got. Never. And if I went in with my hands in my pockets, they would know the job had gone wrong, and nothing more would be said.

If I had that smile on my face and was rubbing my hands, I would walk up to the bar and there would be a drink there, waiting for me on the counter. I would never rush it. 'Nice day,' I'd say.

'Yeah, it's nice,' they'd say, taking it nice and easy.

If you came back with ten grand, say, then you would give them a grand, but they would leave that to you. They would never ask and they were never greedy, but you paid because there was always a next time and their information was good. They didn't run any brasses themselves, but they used to talk to the girls around King's Cross, Knightsbridge and Shepherd's Market, and always knew what was happening.

There was one job I done over Seymour Place. They told me this prostitute had three grand tucked away inside her flat. She had been a naughty girl and had done someone a bad turn, not the Krays but a friend of theirs, and they put me on to her. I twirled her door and got in. She had a little white poodle dog which went yap, yap, yap, so I shut him in the wardrobe and starts searching everywhere for the bread, and can't find it. I comes out and goes to a pub across the road and who should I see but my mate Jimmy Riley. He says, 'Did you look in the toilet?' I told him he must be joking, but went back there all the same, lifted up the top of the cistern, and there was the bread, wrapped in a plastic bag. Three thousand quid, as simple as that, and then I remember the dog who's still going yap, yap, yap, and lets him out. I goes back to Jimmy and gives him a monkey. I didn't have a motor then, so I got a cab and goes home.

Next day, about half past eleven, I goes down to the Grave Maurice. Ronnie says to me 'Was it any good?'

'I couldn't find it,' I says.

'I think you're telling me lies.'

'I didn't fucking have it,' I told him.

'You've got it.'

'All right,' I says. 'I'll be back in a minute. I'm going for a shower.' Then I goes to Stepney Green, has the shower, and comes back to the Grave Maurice, where they're still sitting at the table. Ronnie gives me a little slap. 'You fucking had it,' he says.

'What?'

'You had it!'

'This is embarrassing,' I said.

'Why haven't I seen it?' he says. 'Give me a long 'un,' which is only a hundred pounds.

'Give us about ten minutes then,' I said. I had borrowed a car that morning, and left some money in a carrier bag, goes outside, pulls out a long 'un and a bit more besides. 'Here, cop that,' I tells him. Ronnie pops it in the bin, and says, 'Give us a tenner.' So then two fivers come out.

'How much did you get?' he says.

'There wasn't no three grand there, boy,' I says. 'THERE WAS NO THREE GRAND!'

But Ronnie knew. Ronnie knew every stroke I had done, and then he said to me, 'Jimmy Riley was with you.' Now the funny thing was they didn't like Jimmy Riley. He was a good twirl man, like me, but once he had had a bit of information down Knightsbridge, had a tickle, and never come back. He must have got carried away. Had he made another step like that they would have had him put down.

'Yeah, but he didn't go up to the flat. I went in alone.'

'But you had it!'

'Well, it wasn't no three grand.'

'How much was it?'

'About £1,200.'

'Give me another £200, and we'll call it quits.'

The best times were when we had the El Morocco. I would walk in, having done a job, smiles all over my face, and Ronnie would say, 'Here comes the Colonel.' And I'd say, 'You're the Colonel with a "C", and I'm the Kernel with a "K"', which no one else would have dared to say because C is the word for cunt. 'I'm the Kernel of The Nuts,' I'd say, and they'd always roar with laughter.

The El Morocco was the largest club they ever had. Whenever we went there, we were always clean. We left our shooters and tools outside, in a toilet or whatever, so that the Old Bill wouldn't know whose they were. There were four stairs down into the restaurant, and then the middle table was ours. That was where the firm sat. No one else was allowed to sit there. You never had to go to the bar and order a Scotch. There were always plenty of bottles on the table. Now I'm not interested in too much meat, but sometimes I'd have a minute steak with a poached egg on top, mushrooms, tomatoes, and a bit of salad on the side.

Early evening, Reggie and Ronnie would be walking around the building. There was this restaurant and dance floor on the ground floor with a small stage, three cocktail bars upstairs, and then another, smaller restaurant on the top floor. They would always be wearing dinner jackets, with black bow ties, looking smart, and anyone who came to the club had to look smart as well. All the villains had to wear collars and ties, because that was only showing respect, and if someone new came to the club without a tie, either Ronnie or Reggie would go up to them, always very politely, and say, 'I'm sorry, sir. You're not properly dressed. You have to wear a collar and tie.'

Sometimes you'd get these Jack the Lads in, drunk, or not knowing what they were into, and they'd stand on the step, arguing, shouting or swearing. The Krays wouldn't stand for that. Many times I have seen Ronnie handle that sort of situation, always the same way. He would stand there quietly, listening to this Jack the Lad, and then you would see him start to stroke either side of his chin with his right hand, which you knew meant he was measuring the chap up, deciding where to land the punch, and then WHAM! In would go the left and he'd be down on the deck. No messing!

You had to walk down four steps into the main restaurant where there were dancers and cabaret. David Essex appeared there sometimes before he was well known, and they were always booking Peters and Lee who were old friends. Lennie Peters was an East End boy, and they had done a lot to help him in his career. Late at night, when the West End shows had closed, a lot of actors, artistes and musicians used to come down for a meal or a drink, and the boys had the idea of bringing the film star George Raft into the country. He was an old man then, but they wanted him to become the host at the El Morocco because they thought that his presence would encourage a lot of other show business people to use the club as well. I'd known George Raft over in New York State in the fifties, when he was running a gambling club, and he was good at that sort of role; he had worked for the Mafia and was always so smart and polite. He would have given the El Morocco a lift, which was what they wanted.

One night the firm were all gathered around our table, and Ronnie said: 'We've got George Raft coming over. We want to entertain him and we need some bread, so we're gonna have a whip-round ...' and that night we raised £4,000 for George, in cash, just passing round the hat. Next day, Reggie and Ronnie went out to Heathrow Airport to meet him off the plane, but the immigration authorities wouldn't let him into the country. We didn't realise it but the Old Bill were closing in, and they'd put the blockers on it.

By then the El Morocco had become a meeting place for many of London's top villains and the Old Bill must have known it. Chopper Knight used to come down and he was a good friend to all of us. Chopper would never part with money. When he had done a big job, he would lay the money down and not touch it. He was careful, and that was the trouble because other people on his firm used to go off and do jobs on their own and that was how he got caught. A young kid, whom we all knew, went off and did a little job just to raise £1,500, then he got captured and his bottle went. This kid's wife phoned Chopper and said she needed some money. Chopper takes £500 round for her and it was a fit-up. The Old Bill was waiting for him with shooters. Chopper had had a good run, though. He had been one of the top tea-leaves for years, and the Old Bill never got near him. He's doing thirty-three years now,[3] and to look at him you would never think that butter would melt in his mouth. He wasn't a loud mouth like me. He was very quiet and polite and would come into the club of an evening, play a game of kalooki, and have a pint of lager or a wee whisky. Ronnie Knight used to come down as well. He was married to Barbara Windsor, and had the A & R Club in the Charing Cross Road. So did his brother John Knight, Frankie Fraser, Freddie Foreman and some of the boys who went on to do the Brink's Mat job, and the other big robberies of the seventies and eighties. We used to know 'em all, but I'm not going to tell you all their names because some of 'em never got captured.

The El Morocco brought us all together. The main thing there was the talk. I never bothered with the music or the dancers. Most evenings I'd sit at the table with my back to the stage. If Reggie or Ronnie had some information, they'd come over and tell us. If someone had to be hurt or given a talking to, they'd just give us a piece of paper with their name and address. You would put it in your waistcoat pocket and away you would go. No messing. It was all very quick. It had to be. I knee-capped four and maimed a few more, but as I've said before, never anyone innocent.

I never, ever, saw Reggie or Ronnie drunk. Their drinks would last a long time. Reggie liked brandy or whisky, always mixed with a Coca-Cola, and Ronnie would sit there with a gin and tonic, steadily diluting the gin. One drink might last him fifteen minutes, or even half an hour, because he would sit there topping it up with the tonic, and sometimes he'd order more tonic but not another gin. They would always laugh at me because one bitter lemon would last me a dozen gins, and when I moved on to the whisky I was always drinking it neat. 'Where did you put it all?' they'd say.

[3] See Chronology.

By the end of an evening, when many of the customers had gone home, Reggie and Ronnie would still be there, now sitting at the firm's table, ties gone, collars undone, but still looking smart, and we'd just sit there talking, having a rabbit, right through the night sometimes, discussing business, how this job should be done or that one given a miss. 'It's a pity there aren't a few more like Little Legs,' they'd say, telling 'em all that I was a great little grafter, which I was in those days.

Had the boys carried on like that, sticking to their clubs and protection, which was what they knew, they would have been all right. The Old Bill would never have caught 'em. But they allowed things to get personal.

How the boys went wrong was that people were having a go at them. Other gangs, like the Richardsons, wanted to move in on their manor. People were saying, 'You think you can take care of me?' and all that. 'You're the Kray twins and you think you're the greatest?' People were winding them up, and they were falling for it. Those things would end up with Reggie or Ronnie giving them a backhander, or a left, and then they would get the message, but sometimes it got worse than that.

Normally, the boys led a quiet life. That was the way they were. They didn't go out looking for trouble. They were very polite, very quiet. We would meet down at the Grave Maurice late mornings, like clockwork, have a nice drink, go up to the West End in the afternoon, and then often they would take in a show, 'cos they loved going to the theatre, especially musicals and concerts, and often went to the London Palladium, Her Majesty's Theatre and the Prince of Wales. They used to like the sentimental ones – Vera Lynn, Anne Shelton – and we all went down to the Palladium together to see Judy Garland. You would never know how any evening would end; sometimes we would still be talking at 4 or 5 a.m., sometimes later. It always depended what kind of atmosphere we were in – it would just take us over.

For years, the firm were all good buddies and then people started letting them down. They had been trying to get an agreement with the Mafia, but that never came off. They were trying to rush their fences when they hadn't had the education in international crime, and hadn't travelled enough to know how to handle some of the situations that come up when you're working on that level. They didn't know the right way to handle business, and started getting suspicious of people. They had to be, because their own people were letting them down and that was dangerous because some of them knew too much. They would give someone on the firm a job to do, and then sit waiting by the phone for calls that never came, and then they would start to worry. There's only so much you can take of that. You can't have people working on a firm who let you down, and they had begun to realise that some people would crack if the Old Bill got through to them, because the Old Bill wouldn't mind giving 'em a spank if they had to. They were out to get the Krays, and Reggie and Ronnie knew it, but they didn't know how fast the net was closing.

When the Old Bill eventually got them to court, it was for the murders of George Cornell and Jack McVitie, but there were others. As I've said before, Soho was always dangerous and there were always people disappearing. That was nothing new. You would say, 'Where's so-and-so?' and you'd be told, 'He had to go for a walk.' And it was never only the Krays who were doing it, either. There were other villains around, just as dangerous. Their mistake was allowing things to get personal and then dealing with Cornell and McVitie themselves.

If ever anyone had it coming to him, it was George Cornell. I knew him well and I know his brother, who's still living down in Whitechapel. He's a good feller. George had been on the firm and had decided to move across the river and join the Richardsons. The Krays never minded people going to another firm, but there was a way of doing it. You told them what you were planning, and then kept your trap shut. The Krays would always wish you 'good luck'. But George Cornell got very, very cheeky. He started swaggering around the clubs, telling people that he was with 'the heavy mob' now and that the Krays were finished and he started upsetting Ronnie.

Now I had known that Ronnie was a homosexual for years. He had told me so himself. We didn't use the word 'gay' in those days, but we knew that Ronnie liked young men and we accepted it, although I'm not that way myself and neither was Reggie.

At that time Frankie Fraser, who had a firm of his own in North London and was an old friend of Cornell's, was in the London Hospital. He was ill. Frankie had been having trouble with his liver, and Georgie used to come across in the evenings to go and see him because they were good mates, and every time he did he would come over to the Grave Maurice which is just across the street from the London Hospital. He would come in through the door, poke his head through the curtains, and if Ronnie was there he would say, 'All right, poofter?' and blow him a kiss. This upset Ronnie because although he was a homosexual he didn't like people calling him names.

'He'll have to go,' said Ronnie.

This happened several times, and I saw Georgie Cornell do it myself while I was sitting at the table with Ronnie, because down at the Grave Maurice we always sat facing the curtains, never with our backs to the door. And then we got the message that the Richardsons had killed Richard Hart, who was on our firm, in a shoot-out down at Mr Smith's Club in Catford. That night someone came in to the Grave Maurice and told us that George Cornell was having a drink down at the Blind Beggar.

Ronnie left at once. He was driven over to the Blind Beggar, went inside and shot Cornell, and then he went back home, had a bath and got rid of his clothes so that there would be no forensic. When he came back to the

Grave Maurice he said, 'It's been taken care of,' but he was upset and his hands were shaking. And then he disappeared for a while, lying low in a flat in North London. I went round to see him a few times. He stayed indoors, listening to classical music and moping a lot. He was sorry that he had done it, but how can you be sorry with a bloke like Cornell? If someone takes the piss out of you like that, you can only take so much.

With Jack McVitie it was different. He was a wrong 'un and had been grassing us up. We knew it was him and I was there, sitting on the steps, when Ronnie told Reggie that he had to do that one, although I wasn't actually present when Reggie fired the gun. It failed to go off and then he did him with a carving knife. Reggie didn't really want to do it but Ronnie was the stronger. He had the greater will-power, and I heard him say, 'I did the last one. You do him.' McVitie had to go. You couldn't trust him, and when you have someone like that on the firm they have to go because they put you all in danger.

There were a couple more that never came to court. There was Mad Teddy Smith, who was no relation of mine, and Jack Frost, who did a very silly thing. He went after a girl who was already living with another member of the firm. So he had to go. It was the cement mixer for him. Cement mixers had been used by the gangs in Soho well before the Krays came along. No one can ever prove anything. You don't strip them first. You just chuck them into the top of these big cement vats, clothes and all, and then the blades cut them up, and once the cement has set into building foundations or motorway bridges, no one will ever find them. There's nothing left. Some others ended up in cement mixers, too, but I'm not going to tell you their names.

Ginger Marks ended up in the cement mixer as well. The Old Bill never found his body and they never got the people who did it. He was a cousin on my mother's side. I'd known him for years and he used to come round to the house. The trouble with Ginger was that he would go down to the pub and start talking. He was what we call a peanut-flier and would do anything for a £. He came from Mile End and sold old bangers, but he wanted to move into the big time and had plans to nick a load of metal – nickel silver. He ended up putting someone on a bad steer and two people got nicked because of him, so their friends were waiting for him up an alley, shot him in the back with a 12-bore shot gun, put him in a motor and drove him down to the cement box. A lot of people heard that gun go off!

Frank Mitchell was different. We had known him for years. I had been in the nick with him and so had Ronnie. The Krays arranged to get him out of Dartmoor because Frank was afraid that he would never leave gaol, and Ronnie believed that if he did get out, Frank would be able to draw attention to his claim that he was being unfairly treated. Frank had been locked away for most of his life, since the age of 9, and the prison authorities would never give him a date for his release. Ronnie, who had been in a mental home himself, felt sorry for him but I'm convinced now that Frank was mad, genuinely mad. He had extraordinary strength and was built like the Incredible Hulk.

Once he had been released, Frank wrote a letter to *The Times* asking for his case to be reopened. The Krays really thought that would happen but it had all been a huge mistake. Frank was very frustrated. He had been locked up for years and he wanted a bird. We found him two. One came down from Winston's, and I brought him one down from the Latin Quarter.

Frank was staying in a flat down in Barking and I went over to see him a few times. We'd been in Wandsworth together, years before, and when he saw me he'd ask me to stand in the palm of his hand, and then he would lift me up to the ceiling. He was a big man, abnormally strong, but thick. He would say, 'Hello, Roy. Are you all right, Roy. I'm all right, Roy. I'm glad to see you, Roy.'

Then he would bang me on the head, and say, 'I think a lot of you, Roy.'

Frank was a randy fucker, and he was very ungrateful. The boys soon realised that they should never have got him out of Dartmoor. He had become a pest and was putting us all at risk, threatening to leave the flat and go up West to see a few of the friends he had made inside. In the end, Frank became a blanket job. On Christmas Eve, a Transit van was sent down to Barking and he was told that he was being taken down to the country for Christmas. I was in the flat when he left, said 'Goodbye' and heard the shots from the van. He was told to lie down and hide under a blanket, and then shot, but it took ages to kill him. He was a strong man and mad, really mad, and getting stronger, 'cos he was mad. I wasn't there in the van but I heard all about it.

It wasn't innocent people that were getting hurt with all this violence. It was always villains. No member of the public ever got hurt and the villains knew the risks. Georgie Cornell and Jack McVitie must have known the risks they were taking.

Those were the murders that the Old Bill got them for in the end, and on the morning that Reggie and Ronnie were arrested, the police came after me as well but they couldn't find me. I was in Asia but they still spun the house, turning everything over, and I stayed away for a year. When I came back to London in the November, Reggie and Ronnie were still on remand, awaiting trial. I went back home to my wife but was sleeping in the spare room because we had fallen out, and at six o'clock in the morning, two days after I got back, the Old Bill came steaming in through the door, four of them, armed with guns, two of them dressed in plain clothes. The guns were pointed straight at my head. 'Get out of bed,' says one of them.

'What's all this about?' I said.

'You know,' he says.

'You're joking, aren't yer?'

'We know who you are. You're the midget,' he says.

'Well, yeah. I'm a midget,' I says. 'That's bleeding obvious, isn't it?'

'We want you,' he says.

'Leave it out,' I says. 'I've only just come back from Asia. What would you want *me* for?' because there I was standing by the bed with no clothes on, as I always sleep in the nude. 'Do you mind going outside the door while I get my clothes on?' I said, and then I had a wee dram and copped hold of some fags (because you never know when they're gonna let you have any fags), and says, 'Where are we going?'

'Arbour Square,' he says, which is just off the Commercial Road in Stepney. They took me down there, put me in a cell, and then began the interrogation.

'Now you could be a good boy,' says this copper.

'Waddya mean? I could be a "good boy"?'

'We'd like you to give us a bit of information,' he says.

'You can shut up,' I said, 'cos I've been deaf and dumb all my life. Fuck your information. What's the matter with you? What do you want me for?'

'You've been at it,' he says, and then he goes out and another one comes in.

'He's rough,' says this new copper, as if I didn't know the score; the old hot and cold treatment, hard cop, soft cop. 'He's very aggressive,' he says.

'Is he?' I said. 'No problem . . .'

'Well, if you would talk to me . . . would you like a cup of tea?'

'Well, yes, I might like a cup of tea later,' I said, 'but first I am going to tell you something. You get the fuck. That means, fuck off. If you're gonna nick me, then nick me – but just fuck off. I'm telling you nothing,' because I know that once they have charged you they cannot ask you any more questions. They kept me for forty-eight hours and then let me go. They didn't have the evidence.

Chapter 9

When I brought my Karen back to London, I didn't know what to do for the best. She was so little, so sweet. My marriage to Trisha was finished. I knew that. And I had a large house down in Leamington Gardens, Green Lanes, Ilford, which was much too big for just me and a baby.

I have owned two houses in my time. The first was that house in Strone Road, which my mother inherited from Auntie Nell during the war. When Mum died, she left it to me, 'cos she wanted me to have a roof over my head, and I suppose she thought the rest of the family would find it easier to look after themselves. She always loved me, my Mum, God rest her soul, but I was busy at the time, so I said to my brother Harry, who was living in a flat then, 'You can have it, and if you sell it I want a drink out of it ... I want to be on the move.' That was the gypsy in me. I always wanted to be on the move. He and Pat, his wife, didn't have no babies then, but later they sold it to Indians for four-and-a-half grand. That was over twenty years ago and it was worth more then but, anyway, he dunnit, and I shouldn't call him a silly sod because my Harry is a clever boy, really, normally. He's a good fighter, was a good footballer and has a good head. He's not a bad boy, but I heard recently that houses down Strone Road were selling for £258,000, and that made me feel a bit sick.

That other house in Leamington Gardens, I'd had for ages. It was a big place, five bedrooms, and I'd had people renting it. Now when I rent anything, then that's that. When I tell them, it's for four weeks, three months or nine months, then that's it. When I come back, they've gotta go. That is the rule. No nonsense with rent books and the law. When I make a deal, that's it. A deal's a deal, and when they've gotta go, they go.

I lived there for a while with my Trisha, but when the marriage broke up I sold it to a German bird. That must have been in 1964. I sold the house for eight grand.

First of all, I took my Karen round to my sister Elsie who lives in Hillingdon. Her husband had died, but she had three boys to bring up and when I went over to see her, nearly every other day, I tumbled that the boys were a bit jealous of this little girl coming into their home and getting so much attention. So I took her to stay with my brother Harry who was living down in South Benfleet by then, with two children, John and Jane. I stayed there with them for a while, but I could see that that wasn't fair, either, because the children were too young to understand what was happening. They were a little bit jealous, too.

In October 1965, *The Sunday People* ran another story about 'Fate's Final Blow at the Midget,' saying how Karen had been born a dwarf like me, and that I'd decided to bring her up on my own now that my marriage was finished. They had gone down to see Trisha as well, and she had told them:

> Roy was a very difficult person to live with. His size made him want to be generally nasty to people, although in many ways he was a good husband. When I realised I was pregnant I knew deep in my heart that the baby would be like Roy . . . I loved my baby and cared for her as well as any other mother. But I knew that my marriage to Roy could not last. I let him have Karen because I didn't want her to grow up a little person alone in a big persons' world, as Roy had done. I knew she would be better off with Roy, so I stepped quietly out of their lives.

A few days after that story appeared in *The Sunday People*, I was sitting at the table down at the Grave Maurice one morning, with Reggie and Ronnie, when two fellers came in the door. They were big 'uns, and they had been checking me out, having heard that I had taken up the midget wrestling again.

'Are you Fuzzyball Kaye?' one of them said, which was my wrestling name.

'Yeah.'

'Can we have a talk with you?'

Now I'm thinking for the moment that there might be trouble coming, 'cos I'd never seen 'em before in my life, but Reggie said they were OK. He knew 'em, and who'd come into the Grave Maurice in those days unless they knew what they were doing? So I goes outside and has a talk with 'em in their van.

'Are you the midget wrestler?' they said.

'Yeah, that's right.'

'We promote wrestling down at East Grinstead and in Gravesend,' they said. 'Would you mind doing a couple of shows for us?'

'No problem, no problem at all – as long as the bread's OK.'

And that was how I came to meet Tony Granzi, which was his wrestling name, although his real name was Tony Alexander. He and his brother Barry were both in the game and were known as The Granzi Brothers. They told me that their Mum had read about me in *The Sunday People*.

'You've got a little one, haven't you?' says Tony. 'Mum would love to meet you,' and they took me round to their home in Stayner's Road, Stepney Green, which was where I met their Mum and Dad and their sister Sylvia, who later became my second wife. When I met them all for the first time in October 1965, Sylvia was 23 and I was just coming up to my thirty-fourth birthday, but we didn't start going together until long after that.

When they saw my Karen, her Mum and Dad fell in love with her. They made such a fuss of her and asked if there was anything they could do to help. Well, to cut a long story short, Karen and I both moved in with them, and they became, more or less, foster parents, although I was living there, too, sleeping on a settee in the living room.

Jack Alexander was a diamond of a geezer. He was working lorries, picking up fruit and veg and taking it to the markets, but he had a bad back. His spine had been injured and he wore a belt. For a year or two I had a secondhand car business, until I lost it all one Saturday afternoon gambling on the horses, doubling up on each bet trying to get my money back, and ending up losing the lot. Jack helped me with the cars, doing the resprays, rubbing them down, filling the rust-holes with fibre-glass, and then spraying 'em. These weren't bent cars. I've had bent cars, but this was legit. I didn't think so much of his wife, Leah Alexander – I've never got on too well with my mothers-in-law – but I will say this for the old lady. She was marvellous with Karen, like a real Mum. She used to take her up to the Waste, the market in Whitechapel, buying her little dresses, and thought the world of her.

Even when I wasn't sleeping in the house, I still used to see Karen nearly every day, and taught her everything she knows, wrapping her legs together with bandages when she was a baby so that she wouldn't grow up bandy, just like my mother had done for me. I also taught her sign language and Gypsy backward-talking. She went to school in Morpeth Road, but I taught her the facts of life. Told her she must be careful and mustn't be rude. 'Be nice and kind; that's all you've gotta do, pet,' I used to tell her, and she was never demanding or greedy. When I asked her what sweeties she wanted brought back from the pub, it was always Smarties.

I taught her to read and write, not with books, but with writing on a pad. I taught her the alphabet and how to make up words, and then taught her to type and that backwards-talk, which always comes in handy, because we can talk to each other now without people knowing what we're saying.

Karen's a couple of inches shorter than me, but she's all right on top. Five years ago, she had a little boy who lived three and a half hours, God bless his soul. Then she and her husband George had another little baby, my Georgina, but George is dead now. Died of cancer. Karen was small and she had what you call a chip on the shoulder. She wanted a big black. I've been married three times, counting Heddy, who was a common law wife, but George was no bigger than me. Know what I mean? Karen's now got a flat over Notting Hill Gate and has a spade club down Ladbroke Grove. All the black boys think the world of her.

When she was a kid, I used to buy her lots of toys and then when she was 8 or 9 the decimal coins came out and she saw these 50p coins, and said, 'I'm not going to school until I've had one of those ones with the funny edges.' I've been able to get her a bit of gold over the years. She's got plenty of chains, rings and bracelets, and so has my little one, Georgina. Although I'm skint at the moment, I've looked after them down the years.

When she was little, we used to have a mynah bird in the house down at Stayner's Road, and every time I put my coat on the bird would say, 'There you go. Out on the piss again. Fuck off. Fuck off,' and it was difficult getting out of the house. Sometimes I'd pick up my coat and try and creep through to the hall without the bird seeing me, but just as I was putting my coat on outside, off he'd go. 'There you go. Out on the piss again. Fuck off. Fuck off,' and when I came back from the pub he'd say, 'Pissed again, pissed again.' We had to get rid of him in the end because he was a bad influence on my daughter.

When I first moved into the house, Sylvia was engaged to a lifeguard named Nick who worked down at the Victoria Park baths, and I'd never really thought she'd fall for me. She was an attractive girl and there were other men who fancied her. Ginger Marks used to come round to the house, making a nuisance of himself, and her brothers had to give him a slap.

And then one night we're out somewhere and Sylvia asks me to drop her home. I had me motor car, so I said, 'All right,' and as we get home to Stayner's Road, she says, 'Will you wait a minute?'

'All right,' I says, and she comes straight back out again.

'Where are you going now?' she says, and I tells her that I am thinking of driving over to West Ham.

'Can I come with you for the ride?' she says.

Well, the thoughts start going through my mind, and I says, 'OK – but you ought to know I do naughty things.'

'That's all right,' she says. 'I want you.'

So we didn't go to West Ham after all. I took her to a club in Berwick Street, all blacks, where I'm the ace, and once the blacks see Sylvia, a white girl, they're all at her. She says, 'Can I have a hamburger?' so I takes her round the corner, and it's all a novelty, a big deal, going up the West End and having a hamburger. She says, 'I'm taking my ring off and giving it back.'

Later that night I takes her back home to Stayner's Road again, and she's standing in front of the mirror, combing her hair. You know what women are like: if theirs is straight, it's gotta be curly – and if it's curly, it's gotta be straight. I was looking at her, and looking at her legs, and says 'Hey, pet. You're getting me at it!'

'Can we go for another ride?' she says.

'At this time of night?' I said, because it was now well past midnight, maybe two or three o'clock in the morning. Well, I only had an Anglia but you can imagine what I done. Kiss and cuddle. Sweet as a nut. And that was how we got involved.

When she takes back the ring, Nick gets jealous, refuses to have it and says he wants to fight me. *Wants to fight me!* Me! 4ft 2in. – and him over 6ft! Well, unfortunately, he come unstuck. I did him with an iron bar on Stepney

Green as people were coming out of the flats. 'You'll kill him,' they were saying. 'Royston, stop it,' they were shouting, because they all know me. He ended up in Mile End Hospital, and the next day I told Sylvia to get me a rose. There was a flower stall round the corner. I goes to the hospital and there's the Old Bill, sitting outside his ward. I walks in and he sees the rose in me hand, and being little he lets me through, as they always do, but I've got something else in me pocket. A razor.

Nick is lying there in bed as I walks through. 'Are you all right, son?' I said.

'You hurt me,' he says, and I had. I always do the knee-caps first, because then they can't walk. Once they're on the ground, it's easy after that.

'Look,' I said. 'Here's a present for you,' and gave him the rose, 'but if you grass me, there's something else . . .' and showed him the razor.

'It's all over now, isn't it?' he says.

'Yeah, son. It is.'

'Will I get better?'

'Maybe,' I says, but when I knee-cap someone I do it for life. Look at the size of me! I don't ask for help!

I was still into all kinds of villainy, whatever came along, but nothing too big because of my size. Had I done anything too big, the Old Bill would have captured me straight away because they'd always know where to look. One Friday I went down to this rag trade factory in Hackney and asked for a job. I didn't want a job. This was just me clocking the place over, and there I am standing there, talking to this geezer, and clocking these wage packets standing on a desk. Two trays of 'em. He tells me I'm too small to work there, but I still says, 'Thank you very much for seeing me. I do appreciate it,' and goes back down the steps, stone steps they were.

'We're gonna have it,' I says to my mate Jimmy who was waiting outside. Now I don't like mugging people and I don't like hurting innocent people, so we waits until this geezer has left his office and then we're in, take his briefcase, fill it with the wage packets, and away. That was £2,000 in the bin.

Another trick was bent motors. If you went out of town you used to keep an eye open for cars and then when you saw the sort you wanted, you'd make a note of the number plate. When you came back to London, you would get another number plate made with the same number, and then switch that to a bent motor. That meant that there were two motors on the road with the same number plate, but the odds were on your side that the drivers would never meet – and the Old Bill would never match them up, either. If they phoned up the registration office, they would find that the number matched the motor. That was what we called 'Ringing' in the car trade, and it's so easy.

When I married Sylvia, I had to get my birth certificate and the decree absolute to prove that my divorce from Trisha had all gone through, and that I was free. Three days later we were married. It only cost three-and-a-half quid.

I married Sylvia the day after Guy Fawkes Day, 1967, down at the register office in Philpot Street, Stepney Green, and then just a week later I disappeared, went to Asia. A good offer came through from Boots Productions, a German company based in Bavaria. I met the promoter at the Regent Palace Hotel and he gave me £550 in readies to buy a ticket, and then I went to Air India in Piccadilly, bought a ticket to Tokyo, and went out to the airport, where I phoned Sylvia. They had told me they needed someone to fly out there straight away.

'Where are you?' she said.

'Heathrow Airport.'

'Where are you going?'

'I'm going to Asia.'

This guy had told me there was work in Seoul, South Korea, but first of all I had to get there. He had given me the readies so I knew he must be genuine. I had no idea then how long I would be away, and didn't think of asking her to be faithful to me. Why should I? That's not my way. I'm a very honest man in my relationships with women. I was the same when the women came to visit me in prison. I would tell 'em, 'Look. I'm in here and you're out there. If you fancy a geezer, watch what you're doing. Have a kiss and a cuddle and enjoy yourself . . .' and then the bleeding tears would come. 'Stop it!' I'd tell 'em. 'Enjoy yourself, because I've got bird to do, and I'll be home shortly.' What can I do if I'm doing bird? Play with myself? Well, I'm not gonna do that, but what's good for the goose is good for the gander. As long as they don't bring nothing back, I don't care. All my women were like that, especially Sylvia. Well, she knew I hadn't a chance when I was in the nick, and when I came back from Asia she didn't ask me what I'd been up to and I didn't ask her. So long as they have a nice little dimple on their cheeks when I kiss 'em, I'm not worried.

When I took that job in Asia, I hated the Germans. I was prejudiced because they'd killed a lot of my family during the war, but no one knew I was Jewish until the plane arrived in Cairo. When the hostess saw my Star of David, she said, 'Don't get off the plane with that around your neck.'

From there I flew to Bangkok, then Tokyo, but couldn't get a visa into South Korea, so I flew on to Osaka. They wouldn't give me one there either, so I flew to Hong Kong, got one, and then caught a plane to Seoul where Boots Productions had told me there was work for me, midget wrestling and the trampoline. I had to do a lot of talking when I got there, but I was booted and suited and I'm game.

In Seoul they had a curfew on, and I was staying in this poxy hotel. At night I would go outside and sit on the steps. All of a sudden, twelve o'clock comes and the siren goes, telling everyone to get off the street. A military jeep comes out. 'What's the matter with you?' they say, and I tell 'em that I'm tired. In India and Thailand it's hot, but down in South Korea and Indonesia it's wet and humid, and you sweat all the time. I used to sit there with a little battery fan in one hand and a bottle of bourbon in the other.

'You should be indoors.'

'I can't. It's too hot.'

'Where do you come from?'

'London.'

'Where are you going now?'

'I'm sitting here.'

'We like you. Would you like to come down to our club?'

So they take me down to this club at the German Embassy, weigh me in, and give me everything I want, and then in the motor coming back they take out their machine guns. One sits in the driving seat with a gun across his knees. I'm in the middle, and then this other geezer sits the other side, also with a machine gun. Now, I love a gun. I'm crazy about shooters. But here I am, sitting in a jeep in South Korea, thousands of miles from home, and they start firing into the bushes and I'm wondering where the hell I'm going, while they're taking shots at people who haven't gone home. Next morning, they picked me up again, took me down town to get my hair cut, and while I'm sitting there in the barber's chair, out come the guns again. This time, they're shooting at bits of plastic, just practising. Every time the gun went off, the barber's hand jumped, and he was handling an old-fashioned cut throat razor.

'Leave it out,' I said, and went to get a taxi, but they're not like our taxis. These are tri-shaws, which are pedalled unlike the rickshaws in Japan, where someone pulls you. We're going down the road, when the driver says, 'I'm sorry, sir, but we've got to pull over for a minute . . .' And then just as we're standing there, guns start firing from houses on both sides of the road, and we're caught in the middle of the road. And they say Soho's dangerous! We stay there until the military police come along to sort it out, and then the driver takes me down to another bar and tells me the name of a better hotel where I can stay the night. I go down there, ask for the bourbon, and then say, 'Can you do me another favour? Have you any pretty girls?'

'I'll send one up for you,' he says. Now what you have to do is leave your bath towel on the bottom of the bed, and then when the girl comes into the room she sees the towel and knows what you want. That was the same with the girls down in Macon, Georgia, and in Indonesia, which I moved to next, and where many of the people were of Dutch descent. Then I moved on to the Philippines, staying about two miles from Manila, where I pulled this lovely bird.

'You're cute,' she says, which is what they've always said, and to be honest with you, she was a brass, a prostitute, but once I'd had my leg over she says, 'You don't want to leave me, do you?' and takes me home to meet her Mum and Dad, and her little sister. She was good looking, pretty, and told me the story of how she had become a prostitute. That didn't bother me. 'You've gotta do what you've gotta do,' I said, 'but you've gotta keep yourself clean.' They didn't have a bathroom, so before going to bed she would heat up a saucepan of water, and we'd splash it all over ourselves, always making sure we were clean, and then do the business, sweet as a nut.

The last time we make love, I says to her, 'I've gotta leave. I've gotta go to Bangkok,' and she tells me that she doesn't want me to go. Well, anyway, I catch the plane and I'm on my way to Thailand – this was in 1968, being paid cash in hand wherever I went – and I've changed all my money again into dollars, because I do love the dollar. I've always felt safe with dollars in my pocket. And here I am now arriving in Bangkok, and I've left her behind and, remember, she's a prostitute. That's her living, and

I'm booked to do a show. I stepped into the ring and there she was at the ringside.

'How did you get the money?' I asked her, which was a silly question in all the circumstances, but we books into a hotel and stays there together until it's time for me to go home to England. 'Can I come home with you?' she says. Well, I had to tell her that I was married and how the bleeding hell could I take Felice home to London. I'd only said I was going for three months at the most, but I'd been gone for a year.

And I'd done some crazy things. Out in Jakarta I'd taken marijuana, the real stuff. They had this river which they had the cheek to call the river Thames. They shit in it, piss in it, and then wash themselves in it, and also fish for these small octopuses which live in there too. When they catch 'em they lay them out on the pavements which are so hot that the octopuses dry like crisps, and they sit there, selling 'em, more or less cooked because of the heat, and you can eat 'em just as they are. You can also buy rice cakes, cigarettes and marijuana. These fellers roll 'em while you wait. You choose your tobacco leaf and then they roll it for you with the palms of their hands across a table-top.

That was strong stuff, but I haven't taken any since. Even when I was in the nick I didn't take it, although I sold it. That was when I was getting little bottles of liquid cannabis, and then I'd wipe this down the inside of a fag paper and roll 'em up – not for me, I was on the whisky, but selling 'em, maybe a fiver's worth at a time. The other gear, the strong cannabis, was going for £20. Ordinary tobacco made £10 an ounce.

Out in Jakarta you could get marijuana cigars for ten pence a time and they'd blow your head off if you didn't know how to handle it.

One night, there I was doubled up with pain, and called a doctor. He wouldn't look at me until he had been paid in advance. He didn't want local currency, rupiahs. He asked for US $20, and as soon as he saw that I had it he put me on a bleeding drip. It was only glucose. I've had that many times, but you have to lay there for two hours. 'Shall I come back and see you tomorrow?' he asked. Well, you can imagine what I said. If you drink a lot of Scotch and have no food, glucose does you a power of good. When I'm drinking, I forget about eating. Fags and whisky are all I really live on, apart from the odd boiled egg or a sandwich.

There were a couple of English girls working out in Jakarta with us, and they went up the street to a market. The Asians wanted to look at their boobs because most Asian women don't have big tits, and they haven't seen white girls before. Those men had never seen anything like it, so as the girls walked through the market the men just ripped off their dresses. When they came back, I told 'em, 'I warned you – don't go out on your own, you silly cows.' After that they were scared to go out at all.

I tried to phone home a few times but it was hard work, especially phoning from South Korea, because you had to book the call in advance in those days and then sit by the phone for hours, waiting for them to put you through and call you back. When you got through you'd say, 'Hello,' and then there'd be no reply.

'Hello,' you'd say again, and then if you were lucky, the wife would say, 'Hello.'

You'd say, 'Are you there?,' and she'd say, 'Hello,' and that was costing you dollars.

The first thing she would say every time would be, 'When are you coming home?'

I'd say 'What?' and then the phone would go down, and it would have cost me sixty dollars for nothing.

I brought back a few souvenirs, a sword-stick, a bow and arrow, a pair of curving knives, but if I'd been really clever I would have brought back a load of cannabis. That's where the money is, but I've never been into that, apart from that little bit of business I did in prison. Those cigars were cheap and strong. Smoke one of those right through to the end and you were out of your box.

When I did come back Sylvia was upset because I hadn't phoned her more often, so I went down to the pub and I'd only been back a few hours and these two CID officers walked in and recognised me at once.

'Are you all right?' one of them says.

'Yeah, sweet as a nut.'

'Do you want a drink?'

'Nah,' cos I would never take a drink off the Old Bill. I would buy them one, but never, ever let them buy me one.

'Howd'ya have that tickle?' All right was it?' one of them says. They must have known I'd done another jewellers just before I went away, but they couldn't prove anything. I knew that.

'What are you talking about?'

They said nothing more and we left it at that. I always had a job going in those days, but it was never on the spur of the moment. I always had money in hand, kept a float, and then waited until the right information came along. Always buried the money if I didn't need it. That was safest. Never trust banks. They're worse than villains.

The worst thing I ever done was in Jersey. I had gone over there with that mate of mine, Jimmy Riley. He was a grafter, bless his cotton socks. We got over there and I hit this hotel. Took the bread, about £870, all in readies, but the jewellery was worth more than the bread, so I thought I'd better lose it. The readies were OK. Used notes. No one would ever trace 'em if we were stopped walking through Customs, but that jewellery was dodgy. Must have been worth a couple of grand at least, so I buried it, and went back to Jersey again after I'd come back from Asia, and you'll never guess what had happened. They had covered the bleeding site with concrete, and were building on it. A bleeding block of flats.

Chapter 10

My only regret is that I never became a star. Mine has been a wonderful life, travelling to most parts of the world except Australia, New Zealand and South America, working the streets without illusions. Although not proud of some of the things I have done, I know my life could never have been lived any other way. When you are born with my deformity, you just have to make the best you can.

Most people look on me as just a freak of nature, but never the villains and those who work in show business. They have always accepted me for what I am. In both fields you are judged only by what you can do and how well you can do it. Class and race count for nothing, and that's the way it should be, in my view. As the Krays used to say, I've been a great little grafter, the very best, and I've never been idle. Every morning there's been something new to turn to. I have never stopped learning.

But there's still been that one regret. I would have loved to have been a star, because I'm sure I could have handled it, before the whisky took such a hold on my life.

As it is, I have had to settle for forty years spent appearing in pantomime, busking on the streets of London, playing the dwarf or the jester in films and television, turning my hand to anything, like midget wrestling, spivving, poncing, working my barrows or touring in circus, but never seeing my name up there in lights. That's been a frustration because I've worked with everyone.

Out in the States I appeared in that film *Trapeze* with Burt Lancaster, met Brando, Sinatra, Dean Martin, Bing Crosby, John Wayne, and here I've made two films with Elizabeth Taylor, and appeared with the Beatles in *Magical Mystery Tour*.

Elizabeth Taylor and me just don't get on. I can't stand the cow. I met her first when she was filming *Beau Brummel* with Stewart Granger, down at Pinewood. I had been booked to play the usual part, court jester, and what I had to do was jump out of a cake at a party and then take a tumble, but when the time comes and I'm supposed to be shooting my scene she's still pissing about – rabbit, rabbit, rabbit – so I goes over to the bar, gets a drink, sits down and lights a fag.

She starts shooting her scene again, and then she stops, on camera, comes over to me and says, 'Do you mind not smoking?'

'Fuck off, yer slag!' I says, and I'm upset. I've got the needle. I goes back to the bar and starts drinking, and I'm supposed to be on next. Stewart Granger comes into the bar, bless his cotton socks. I think the world of that man.

'Come on. Let's have a talk,' he says.

'Waddya mean?'

'Well, you speak your mind, don't you?'

'That's what it's for,' I says.

'Cool it,' says Granger, and takes me over to the canteen, buys me an egg on toast, and calms me down.

'Listen,' I says. 'I don't let no one wind me up . . .'

'She was carried away,' he says, quietening me down, and explaining that this was a difficult scene and that she had had to shoot it again to get it right.

I made another film with her, *Black Lady*, with Dennis Price, a right poof, although I liked the guy, and then some years later met her again in Dublin, late at night and quite by chance. I had gone over there to do the midget wrestling and was staying at the Gresham Hotel in O'Connell Street. Richard Burton was staying there as well, and he was a mate of mine. He often used to come down to the Kismet Club and the El Morocco. It was three o'clock in the morning and we'd been drinking for hours, with me telling him stories about the wrestling game, when Liz comes down the stairs. 'You're corrupting him,' she says. *Me* corrupting *him*!

I met Peter Sellers when I was working at the London Palladium. He was like Harry Secombe, a comedian on stage and off. So was Sid James, God rest his soul, whom I worked with in two Palladium pantomimes. Sid was a diamond, a gambler and a drinker. I used to go and place his bets for him and then bring back the booze.

Arthur Askey and Roy Kinnear had the rooms next door, with Frank Ifield and Kenneth O'Connor the other side. On Wednesdays and Saturdays we did matinées, and then I'd be in Sid's dressing room all day, sitting on me bum and having a wee dram while Sid put his bins on to write out the bets. Because I had a longer break than he'd got I'd go round the corner, opposite the stage door and down Carnaby Street, to place the bets.

Sid thought the world of me. He had a daughter the same age as Karen, but he didn't like his wife to see him gambling or at the drink. Sometimes George, the stage door-keeper, would pop his head round the door and say, 'She's on her way.' And then whoooosh! We would tidy up the racing papers and whisk all the bottles into Arthur Askey's room next door, and then out would come the air freshener to make his room smell nice. Arthur never drank and never smoked. I used to think he was a miserable man until I realised that his wife was ill. I thought he was being offish because he was top of the bill and I was right down the bottom until I heard that he had those troubles, and then I was choked. To be honest, I cried. The guy who told me was Sid Morrison, who worked for Lew Grade, and in later years worked for Cliff Richard and The Shadows. There was nothing I could say, so after that whenever I saw him coming in the stage door I'd say, 'Afternoon, Arthur.'

'Afternoon, Jimmy,' he would say, because my name then was Jimmy Kaye.

I didn't like Frank Ifield. He was a good performer, but I didn't like his attitude towards other artistes. Normally, when you do a pantomime there's a happy feeling in the show and you all come together on the last night and give each other presents. He gave me a glass tankard with his name engraved upon it, and it said –

FROM FRANK IFIELD TO JIMMY

I threw it at him.

During that Frank Ifield pantomime I got into trouble again with the Old Bill. I still used to have me barrows outside in Argyll Street, and one night I done two people over. That was in the February. I stabbed one of them and was charged with causing actual bodily harm. I can't tell you what it was about, even now, because other people were involved, but there had been a rip-off, and when someone tries to rip you off there has to be a come-back. I had to use a blade. Look at the size of me. But it wasn't serious. I gave him one up the belly 'cos I only wanted to hurt him; you can't get killed if you're stabbed in the belly. If you want to kill a geezer, you go up top. The case took a long time to come to court and when it did I got eighteen months. They let me out of Wandsworth in less than a year, and that night Reggie and Ronnie threw a 'Welcome Home' party at the El Morocco. I was the only one who didn't have to wear a collar and tie. That was in June 1967, just before I filmed *Magical Mystery Tour* with The Beatles.

That was down in Shepton Mallet, and as soon as he sees me Paul McCartney comes over and says, 'I'm glad you could come.' It was a bitterly cold morning, and there I was jumping from foot to foot, rubbing my hands. 'Where's the bar?' I said. All they had was tea and coffee, so Paul pops me into his Roller and drives me down to the nearest pub, which was shut. But that doesn't bother him. He knocks on the door, and of course the landlord knows him, doesn't he? Everyone knows Paul McCartney.

'Would you please look after my friend,' he says, and the landlord takes me into the bar, sits me down, and I'm there drinking whisky until twelve o'clock when they call me for my scene. I was a bit wobbly that day, I can tell you.

The first of the pop stars I ever met was Wee Willie Harris, who used to appear at the 21's coffe bar in Old Compton Street. That was before he dyed his hair red. He was only a short geezer. The 21's was owned by a mate of mine, Paul Lincoln, who was also a wrestling promoter. Tommy Steele, Cliff Richard and Terry Dene all appeared there in the old days, and I used to go down there nearly every night, and then I went over to Hamburg at one stage. That was in 1961 or 1962 when The Beatles were appearing there at a club called The Indra. That was where I first met Paul, who always has a word whenever he sees me around Soho, 'cos he has his offices in Soho Square.

I've worked with Cliff Richard many times, and toured with him once for fourteen months, going round all the ABC Theatres. It was Kay Lester who got me jobs like that. Whenever I was away in prison, she would always write and let me know what was coming up and she'd try to have work lined up for me when I came out. A lot of those jobs came through Lew Grade, whom I'd known for years ever since I'd worked with his wife Kathleen Moody in *Babes in the Wood*, at Aston Hippodrome. I could always go and see Lew any time I wanted to; he was always good to me.

They call him Lord Grade now, but I don't. He's 'Lew' and his wife's 'Kathleen', because I'd never call anyone Lord. I don't believe in all that class stuff and titles.

Once, I got hold of a load of lighters. They looked like cameras, but they were cigarette lighters and I sold a couple to Kathleen's brother Les, who was a photographer. 'My husband would like one of those,' she says, so I went round to Lew's office at 501 Regent Street, and there he was, sitting at this huge desk with this fat cigar. 'Give him a drink,' he says as I walk in the door, and then he passes me an envelope, which was a nice way of doing it, never having to handle the cash, just like the Krays. Whenever I did a little job for him there would always be twenty quid in the envelope.

Years later, only two years ago, after he had lost that TV empire he had, I saw him walking across the road to his car. His chauffeur was standing there, holding open the door, and I was on the pavement, drawing pavement pictures. This was at Marble Arch. He gets in the car and they're just leaving when he sees me and tells the chauffeur to stop. 'It's Jimmy Kaye, isn't it?' he says, and he tells the chauffeur to phone through to his office on the car phone, and there was another twenty quid waiting for me in an envelope. 'Give Kathleen a kiss for me,' I said.

The first time I worked with Cliff Richard was nearly thirty years ago. Every night I'd walk into their dressing room, and they'd be sitting there, with Cliff strumming away at his guitar; that was when he was just beginning to work with The Shadows. I always had a wee dram, but they didn't drink, apart from Jet Harris, who couldn't handle it. Tony Meehan was a terrific drummer, but Jet would never have made the grade. He was married to a nice girl from up North, his first wife, and she was a bit on the tubby side, but Jet wouldn't look after her. He was still Jack the Lad. 'I'm a star, I'm a star', and all that, trying to get off with the chorus girls. I sorted him out in the pub across the road from the Palladium, which used to be the Marlborough Head, but they call it the Dog and Trumpet now. His wife had come down to see him with the kids and there'd been tears, and then he went into the pub and there were strangers in there, and he'd been winding them up. Now in show business you have to take everything cool. You must be polite to people outside the business, because they're the customers who pay your wages, and you never know when they're gonna come back. 'He's well out of order,' said the manager, so I gave him a right working-over. Did him up the belly first, and then the chin, the guts, the lot. It was the same old story. Too big for his boots. I thought I'd be in trouble for doing that, but no one told me I'd done wrong. They all said he deserved it, even the company manager, but he didn't get the message, poor sod. He went solo and then fucked up his career.

In those days, Cliff Richard used to sign an enormous pile of photos every night to be handed out to his fans, and guess who used to nick 'em? I used to take them down the road, give 'em to a tout, and then we'd split 'em down the middle. Good money, good money! Cliff could never get out of the theatre, and he had a lovely little red car, a Sunbeam Alpine, which was always getting scratched to pieces by these kids scratching their names and 'I Love Cliff,' so we used to have a little routine to get him out safely. I would back right up to the door in my old Anglia, and then he'd creep in and I'd drive him off to this hotel near Regents Park, where he was as safe as houses, plenty of security. No one ever thought of looking for Cliff Richard in a Ford Anglia!

I used to think the world of him in those days, but that was before he got into all this religion, and I went off him after that. Even then he used to get upset 'cos people were telling him he was a poofter, but I used to tell 'im, 'Don't worry,' 'cos he was only a kid at the time, and he had this girlfriend Jackie Irving, who later married Adam Faith. I knew him, too. Met him up at Lew Grade's office one day, and he couldn't get over my accent.

'Where are you going tonight?' he said, and I told him I was going down to the Regent Palace to have a drink with Shirley Bassey, who had a suite there at the time.

'Do you know her as well?' he says.

'Bloody right I do,' I told him, and he asks me if I'd take

him down there, which I does, and makes the introduction. Stella Starr was there as well, a black South African singer, and we're all just sitting there, some drinking coffee and me just having a shant, having a nice little rabbit, when this Irish geezer, her road manager, suddenly comes in the door with a shooter and starts going bang-bangs. Well, you can't go on playing with shooters down at the Regent Palace 'cos someone is bound to hear you. Along came the Old Bill who found bullets in the ceiling and the furniture with Shirley sitting there in tears, and he got eighteen months. I mean, if someone walks in the door with a shooter and starts going bang, bang, bang, you've gotta have the horrors, haven't you?

A week later I saw Adam again, same place – down at Lew Grade's office – and he says, 'I don't wanna go through that again!'

'What's the matter, kid?' I said. 'Did your bottle go?'

I was always in and out of the London Palladium in those days, because I'd been in so many pantomimes and had the fruit barrow outside in Argyll Street. Everyone knew me, and I was drinking heavy even then, although I wasn't an alcoholic like I am now. When I wake up in the mornings now I go looking for a drink, and that's an alcoholic, but I still won't drink anything. Normally an alcoholic will drink anything you put in front of him, and you see these guys in here (the St Mungo hostel) who will drink cider, meths or cheap wine, often mixed together, but I won't have that. Just the whisky, although sometimes a barley wine does go down nice.

That's why I've always had to work so hard, 'cos whisky's not cheap and I'm a two-bottles-a-day man, and have been for years, even when I was working in pantomime and variety. I've played more dogs than most people have had hot dinners, and often worked a few months here or a few months there as a stooge or a clown. That was what I was doing with Stan Stennett, The Three Monarchs and the Morton Fraser Harmonica Gang, diving between their legs and messing up the big number; the same with Terry Scott and Hugh Lloyd, when they were playing the Ugly Sisters in *Cinderella*. That was with Cliff Richard, again.

But it's always been small parts, novelty numbers, because of my size. In the BBC TV series *Doctor Who*, viewers never even saw me at all because I was hidden away inside a small machine, playing one of the Chumleys. For that I had to sit on the ground with this specially made machine lifted on top of me. One day I got a huge splinter right up my bum. I threw the top off and my bum was bleeding. I went straight to the bar, got a drink and sat down in the nearest chair.

As I'm sitting there, nursing my arse, up comes the Clicker, the fellow who holds up the clapper-board, and the assistant producer. 'Mr Hartnell doesn't like anybody sitting in his chair,' he says. That was enough for me! I picked up that fucking chair and threw it across the studio! William Hartnell had heard what had happened, and back comes the assistant producer: 'Mr Hartnell apologises . . .'

'You can tell Mr Hartnell that I don't take messages secondhand,' I says, which is right. If I am in the wrong, I will say 'Sorry'. No one ever has to do it for me.

Another time I was appearing down at the East Ham Palace, touring in a variety show with Vera Lynn, when I was attacked by a baboon. This baboon had been working in a pony act, and he was naughty, spiteful, so they kept him in a cage right at the side of the stage. Little Legs here was standing in the wings waiting to go on stage when, all of a sudden, he reached between the bars and got me by the hair, and then started banging my head against the side of the cage. He wouldn't let go. This happened four or five times before I got away. After I'd done my spot I went off and got a banana and showed it to him. 'You ugly fucker,' I said. 'Do you want this?' By then his lips were going, and he was licking them while I peeled it; then I gave it to him. He ate it and handed me back the skin, and as he put his hand through the cage I gave him a slap.

Once I did a TV show with Arthur Haynes, whom I had known for years and years and years. I had worked in variety with him and he used to come down to the Kismet Club. He and I were filmed, standing as doormen outside the Regent Palace Hotel. He is all dressed up and so am I. Along comes a huge car. He steps forward, lifts his umbrella, and out step this couple ... and then along comes a little battery car, I step forward and out jump two dwarfs!

There were always little jobs like that for me to do. I also appeared in *Emergency Ward 10*, and once thought I was going to get my own spot on *Double Your Money*. I had done a pantomime at Edmonton Granada with Hughie Green, and then I was asked if I'd like to appear in the TV show. I turns up at Wembley to film the show, and they show me into a back room where I'm given all the answers to the questions – the first was for £1, the second for £2, the third for £4, the fourth for £8, the fifth for £16 and the sixth for £32. After that you were on your own. You had to find your own answers!

After I had learned all the answers I had to go into the audience with my wife, Sylvia, and then sit there while Hughie Green walks on. Everyone claps, and he says, 'Before anyone can come up on stage I have to ask you a question ... and the first one who gets the answer comes up and appears in tonight's show. Now, can anyone tell me the right name for a foxglove?'

There I am, sitting in the front, with the answers in my pocket, and I shouts, 'Excuse me – I've got it!'

'Yes, sir. What is it?' he says.

'Digitalis.'

There's a round of applause, and I am invited to join him on the stage. 'Leave it out,' I says, because we'd agreed backstage that I should do a moody so that he could plead with me to go up on the stage, which gets *him* another round of applause from the audience.

'I think you're very cute,' he says.

'A lot of people say that.'

And then we go through the questions, but I don't have to give him the answers straight away. I have to appear to be thinking about it, and giving him a bit of the verbals.

'What do you do for a living?' he says.

'Old bangers.'

'Sausages?' he says.

'No,' I says. 'Secondhand cars.' Of course, more applause. That's the name of the game. It's all show business, and right at the end he says, 'I also hear you do midget wrestling?'

'Now and again,' I says.

'If I can bring a wrestler here next week, ladies and gentlemen, would you like to see Little Fuzzy come back here again?' he asks the audience, and there's more applause.

'Don't you bring Mick McManus!' I says.

So, anyway, I'm supposed to come back next week, and I'm told there will be a fee of one-and-a-half – and the next Monday I go back with Stanley, my brother-in-law, who drives me, and I weigh him in for fifty quid. We film the wrestling bit for them, and then they come on the blower and say they won't be screening it so there will be no bread.

'That's not my fault,' I said. 'You booked me, I came, recorded the show – and now I want the dough.'

In the end, they offered me £75. 'That's not good enough,' I said. So then they asks me if I will sell two cars for 'em, 'cos I had a parking lot in those days, selling cars down Roman Road. This was a Jaguar Mark 10 and a Hillman Super Minx. So I sold 'em, sure enough – and kept the money – so the Fraud Squad came down and nicked me. That was me banged up again!

The other time I came unstuck was in Blackpool. I had been booked to appear with Charlie Cairoli at the Blackpool Tower, and I didn't like him at all. That was when I was wrestling with Tommy Gallagher, and his agent told me that Charlie liked our act – it was a good act and we only broke up when he fell in love with that girl. Once they get their leg over, you've lost 'em.

In the act, I always played wicked; you have to have a bad guy and a good guy in wrestling, and Tommy was always nice whereas I was fierce and aggressive. I would climb in through the ropes and go, 'Grrrrrrrrr!' And the audience would be on his side right from the start. In this Blackpool show, they all had a go at me – the seconds, the referee and Tommy all picked me up together and chucked me into the pool at the side of the stage, which was the gimmick we had arranged in advance.

Night after night that went well, and the audience loved it – until one night my head hit the scaffolding at the side of the tank. Luckily, a geezer in the audience saw this happen and jumped in fully clothed and pulled me out, unconscious. That man, God rest his soul, died of a heart attack the following day.

This routine was upsetting Charlie Cairoli who thought I was getting too many laughs. That was something he could never stand. Charlie was selfish. One day someone comes to me on his behalf and says, 'Can we come to an arrangement?'

'What arrangement?' I said, and he told me about Charlie being upset, and that they could recommend me for another bit of business in a wrestling promotion down on the South Shore.

'That's OK, but I want my wages every week,' I said, because we had sixteen weeks to go. That was agreed, and they paid me for the next sixteen weeks to do nothing, which I didn't mind at all. Every Friday I would go down to the office and collect my dough, and then I got paid for doing the other show as well. One week I noticed that there was a flaw in their security: you could walk down the steps to the office on a Friday, press a buzzer, the doors would slide open, and then you could nip straight inside and cop the week's wages without being seen. That looked like a good tickle.

So the following Friday my plans are laid. Down I go, ready to go inside, and the place was swarming with the Old Bill. That feller Sewell had just shot the copper Richardson round the corner, and the Old Bill were everywhere. Bang goes my wages!

Chapter 11

I'll admit it. I've been a waster. Thousands, tens of thousands, have passed through my hands, and now I'm skint. It's all gone.

When I came back from Asia, I tried to go straight for a bit. Ronnie and Reggie were banged up in Brixton awaiting trial. The Old Bill hadn't got anything on me, and the case against them was thin until two of the boys on the firm, Scotch Jack Dickson and Ronnie Hart, turned against them and gave evidence for the Crown, but I still didn't think the twins would go down. I thought they'd get away with it, like they usually did, like they had the last time they were banged up in Brixton, when I had been in there with them. They always had bloody good lawyers.

When the day came for the jury to consider their verdict I went down to the Old Bailey, hoping to be there with them and their Mum when they walked down the steps, but when I sat there in the public gallery and saw the jury file back into court, I knew that they had had it. I could tell that by the expressions on the jury's faces, so I slipped out of the courtroom and sat on the steps, wanting to be alone, 'cos I couldn't bear to see 'em sent down.

The firm kept going for a couple of years after that. The Old Bill didn't capture us all, but with Ronnie and Reggie sent down for thirty years we gradually drifted apart. I tried to go straight, opening a disco for blacks in Bethnal Green, running a couple of pubs – the Alexander in Victoria Park and the White Hart in Lower Clapton Road – and tried selling cars again. I even set up a business washing down pub fronts and my own mini-cabbing firm, Viceroy Cars, but none of it worked for me, though I made thousands again, and was soon back in the nick.

Sylvia and me got back together again, and she had a

hard time when my Simon was born. That was 13 October, 1970. She was in labour a long time, and then he had to be taken out with forceps. For years afterwards, Simon had the shakes. He was very nervous. Now he's a great big tall boy, but he's caggy-handed, left-handed. I don't want him to have the sort of life I've had, but I don't want anyone to take a pot at him, either, so I've taught him how to defend himself, just like my Dad educated me. When he was born, Sylvia's father, Jack Alexander, and me took him out to Israel and lived on a kibbutz for six weeks so that Simon could be properly baptised and circumcised on Israeli soil, but I couldn't bear to hold him while they cut him. Jack had to do that while I slipped across the road for a wee dram. Funny, me being sensitive over a thing like that, after all the things I've done, but I just couldn't handle it. Simon went back to Israel again in 1984, which is our custom, just working on a kibbutz for six weeks, picking fruit. I was back in the nick again at the time. I'd had four months from Bow Street and three months from Vine Street. Only the silly things I do. It's always knuckles. It was just a couple of punch-ups with hot dog barrows. People getting in my way.

Most of my convictions have been for violence. There have been three stabbings and two shootings, but there have been many more that I haven't been captured for. That's 'cos I've never hurt an innocent person. It's always been villains and, mostly, they don't grass. I've had twenty-two convictions, in all, but I reckon I've got away with more than I've been done for. My biggest sentences were a seven and a four. The seven was for a shooting at the Black Cat Club in Kensington when I shot a geezer called Frankie Randall. He died later and I got done for manslaughter. It was him or me. I heard that he had put out a contract on me, so I got in first and went round to the club at dead on ten to three, 'cos I knew its hours were 3 p.m. to 11 p.m.

'You know me, don't yer?' I says, as I gets up on the bar

stool with a .22 in me pocket. I don't usually like using those, 'cos they're for girls, but they're easy to handle.

'Yeah,' he says. 'I've got a message for you,' which is what they say when they're gonna cut you or whatever.

'Yeah,' I says. 'I heard about that. Now, as it happens, I've got one for you,' pulls out me gun, and pop goes the weasel, but I only shot him in the shoulder. Other guns started going off and when I pulled the trigger I fell off the bar stool, which was a daft thing to do, so I missed the second shot, but it was me the Old Bill came looking for, 'cos I'm known. It took them four months to find me 'cos I went down to Berkshire. I've got relatives there, about eleven miles from Newbury, and I went into hiding until I thought things had gone quiet. When I went back home to my wife, the Old Bill picked me up coming out of the house. They'd been waiting for me.

They've never caught me for most things I've done, and I reckon I'm showing a profit. The biggest one that I ever got away with was for £14,000. That was a blag. I saw this geezer coming out of a bank and snatched his briefcase. Easy. Give 'em a push and you've got it. I can't tell you when or where that happened, 'cos they still might nick me – but you can take it from me, that was a good 'un. No one got hurt, and he'd have been covered by insurance.

Another time, I was out with a mate of mine, Tommy Williams. He's dead now, silly sod. Took an overdose of pills with a drink, which is a mug's trick. If I've got a headache I won't take an aspirin or whatever because I know how much alcohol I've got running through my system, drinking a couple of bottles of Scotch a day.

Anyway, we were going up the road to ring a couple of motors and we picked up this Zodiac, which was always a popular car, better than the Zephyrs or Consuls, 'cos they were the flash ones and very popular down the East End. We picks up this Zodiac, drives down past the library, turns the corner, parks the motor and I gets out to have a look in the boot. Inside there's a briefcase. I jumped back in the car and told Tommy: 'No more motors today. We're moving,' and we drove to the other side of Hyde Park. This time we stopped again, and I opened the briefcase – and there was £1,500. We didn't have to go to work again that day! Tommy was so happy he went away for a week. You see, a lot of 'em don't know what money is. Once they've got a handful they're Jack the Lads, millionaires for the day.

After I lost that car site gambling on the horses, I was selling cars at the door and then, all of a sudden, I got another nice little number, handling snatch-backs. That's when you work for a finance company, as an agent, grabbing back cars when people have defaulted on their hire purchase payments. The first job they sent me out on was to snatch back a Bedford Dormobile in Ilford.

I gets a taxi over there, 'cos I realise that I shall probably be driving the Dormobile back. People think I can't reach the pedals, but I always used to carry a suitcase to put behind me on the driving seat and a cushion to cover the pedals. I wasn't the best driver, but I could get by. Anyway, I goes on the door and a black woman comes out. I shows her the papers and tells her who I am.

'My husband knew someone was coming, but we can't afford it,' she says.

'Pet, I'm sorry, but I've got a living to get and that Dormobile now belongs to me,' I said, and she gave me the keys and the log book and I took it back to Stayner's Road. Now, fair play, I did one good thing for her. I parked it, looked in the back and there was a big toolbox and I thought to myself, 'That's his living.' So I put that in me motor and drove back to Ilford to let 'em have it back, 'cos the tools were worth more than the motor. They couldn't thank me enough.

With snatch-backs the finance company lets you have the car for whatever money they want back to make good the loan. If it's a later model, they may come down to take a look at the motor to see what it's worth, but usually they don't even want to see it and they'll let you have it cheap. If the motor was worth more than the loan, they used to pay me for the car – but if it was worth less, then I would pay them. Mostly it was Fords, because that's what the flash boys were always into down the East End.

I have had some aggro with snatch-backs. Youngsters who don't want to lose their motor, and then I had to tell them that no matter what happened I was taking their bleeding motor. When I went to call on them, they could keep the car if they paid up there and then, but I couldn't give them twenty-four hours. Once I had taken the car away, I used to tell them that they could have the car back if they came up with the bread in three days. If not, then I sold it.

When you go out on people's doors snatching back motors, you've gotta have some bottle. You never know what the geezer's gonna do when he comes to the door. Sometimes they come at you with a knife. 'You touch that motor, and I'll do you,' they say, and then you have to talk them down, because you have to get the log book and the MOT as well when you take the motor. And then I used to take them back to Stayner's Road and sell them from outside the door.

Once I was selling a Hillman Minx, which I'd advertised in the *Evening Standard*. Two callers came and said they were interested. 'Is it possible that we can give you a deposit?' they asked.

'All right,' I said, 'but when are you going to give me the rest?' This was on the Saturday and they said they would let me have it on the Monday. On the Monday, they didn't show up so I said to Stanley, my brother-in-law, 'Let's go walkies.' And how do you think we found it? By following the oil spots. Drop, drop, drop down the road to Cleveland Way, Stepney Green, turn left into a yard and there's the motor. Now, I was tooled up; and I mean, tooled up. All of a sudden, this geezer comes out and I says, 'Here you! I want that motor back – or I want the money!' He runs back into his house and brings out a hatchet.

'Son,' I said. 'That won't do you the world of good. It will not do you good. Now, drop it! Do yourself a favour. I do not want to see you hurt. Drop it! Or I will cut you from here to Doomsday . . . I want the car back or the money.'

'What about my deposit?' he says.

'You don't get no deposit back, son,' I told him. 'No way. I let you have that motor in good faith, and you either give me the money that is due or that motor is going back.'

'Can I give you another £20?'

'No. I told you. The money, or I take back the motor.'

So there was a bit of a bust-up. I said to him, 'Well, you've had it, son. I won't call the Old Bill because I don't need the Old Bill. I can take care of my own problems. Do what you've gotta do.'

'Well, to be honest, I can't afford it.'

'Fair enough,' I said, and told my Stanley to get in the motor and drive it back home.

Two or three days later, they come round again and said they had put together a few more quid. 'Now, look. Don't ever try to rip me off again,' I said. 'If you try you are gonna get hurt,' and, fair play, they did come back again a few days later with the rest. They had tried to rip me off, and you can't let people get away with that 'cos if they do it once they'll always try again.

When I had the minicab firm, I used to have Indian drivers, and I also put Sylvia's brother, Stanley, on the firm because he wanted to do the knowledge to become a black cab driver. I gave him a motor and he used to go out cabbing, and I had a controller in the office, running the phones. One day he gets a call from the dockers' leader, Jack Dash. He was only a little feller, but he was their union boss, and he wanted a cab. As it happens my Stanley was out on another job so one of my Indians went round to the Commercial Road to pick him up, and I'm in a pub, the Imperial, in Grove Road, just round the corner in Mile End.

All of a sudden this driver comes in and says: 'We're having a bit of trouble. This man phoned for a cab, and then sent it back,' so I gets off the stool and goes to the phone.

He says, 'I'm Jack Dash!'

'Oh, yeah.'

'I've ordered a cab and I want a white driver.'

'I do apologise,' I said to him. 'I do apologise. I will come myself.' Now Jack Dash didn't know me, and I jumped into my motor and drove round to his flat, which was on the twenty-second floor of this tower block. I couldn't reach the lift button so I goes to the boot of my car and gets the crook-lock out, does the button, and then goes up in the lift, and knocks at his door.

'Who is it?' he says.

'The guvnor.' He opens the door, sees the crook-lock in my hand, thinks I'm gonna smash his head in, and shuts it quick, so I opened the letter-box and said, 'Come on, Jack. It's me, Little Legs. I haven't got this to hit you. I couldn't reach the lift button.' So in the end he comes out, a bit timid, and I takes him to Whitechapel. He gets in the front seat of the car but he's still on tenterhooks, so I throw the crook-lock in the back.

'Why's an intelligent man like you a racist?' I asks him, because I'm not. A man's a man so far as I'm concerned, whatever the colour of his skin.

'I dunno,' he says.

'You've gotta brain, haven't yer? Use your loaf,' I told him, and then when we pulls in he gives me fifty pence.

'What the bleeding hell is that?' I said. 'You've had two trips. We've had to send two drivers,' and then he starts stuttering and saying that's all the change he's got, and then he produces a note, 'cos his bottle has gone, so I let him go. I couldn't be bothered with him. I went back to the office, gave the other driver the fifty pence, and told the controller to tell Jack Dash if he ever phoned again that we had no cars. You don't need people like that. He's dead now, but I'm not going to say God rest *his* soul, the tight-fisted bastard. I'm not being big headed, although I was born with a big head, but I really do have a heart of gold. I waste money. I give it away, and I can't stand people like that. If I have a couple of bob on me, I will always give it away to someone else if they need it 'cos I know I can always survive. Duck and dive, every time.

I was just the same in the nick, and I've been in a good few times now. It's never bothered me. I know I can take it, and every time I've done a job I've always known that if I got captured that's where I'd end up. No problem. Just accept it. That's what you've gotta do. There's still a lot of people can't handle it. How many times have I seen people top themselves? They get the blankets off their beds, rip them up into pieces, and then string themselves up. That happens a lot, but you don't hear much about it because these stories often don't make the papers. No one is ever told, unless they're young or they've got a family. So many blokes are on their own, and then there's no one to tell.

As soon as you go into prison you have to have a bath and then they give you your clothes and take you to your peter, and give you sheets and blankets. I've always slept well in the nick, providing I was on my own, and most days I'd go into another cell and play cards, the four of us. The screws would come round and say, 'It's about time you went to bed?'

'We'll go to bed when we're ready so fuck off,' we'd say, and off they'd go and leave us alone, 'cos they don't want trouble, do they? They're doing time as well. Most nights we'd play cards as late as we like, or I'd go back to my cell and read Westerns and gangster stories. I've read all those Luke Short books, the whole of the Johnny Edge series, and a lot of those Mafia books, especially stuff about Al Capone and Lucky Luciano. I've always liked reading about them. That's how you get through your time. Playing cards, reading, trying to get yourself a good job like tea boy, which gives you a chance to move around the nick dealing in dope or tobacco, never letting anything get on your nerves, because you've just gotta learn to live with it.

A lot of dealing goes on in prison. Tobacco's like money. It's worth a lot. I wouldn't deal in hard drugs, pills or acid, but I used to have a little bottle of liquid cannabis which I'd wipe inside the cigarette papers, and I did very well with that. I often carried £300 or £400 on me in the nick, either sewn inside the belt of my trousers or strapped around my ankle.

I never had any difficulty getting the liquid cannabis. There are bent screws in every nick, and you could always get things in from outside, or messages out. I've organised bottles of whisky, gin, or whatever, and also had another guy who was what we call Number One on the hot plate. He was the guy serving the hot dinners to the screws in their canteen and he'd pick up all their dog ends for me and keep them in a jug so that I had tobacco coming from him as well. You can get nearly everything you want in from outside, except a woman – and I managed that once. I did a moody and said I was sick, so they sent me down to the prison hospital, where I knew they'd let a woman come and see me. She says, 'We can't do anything here!'

'Can't we?' I says. 'We've got an hour!' and I slips a bit of dropsy to the screw who goes outside, locks the door and leaves us to it. He comes back an hour later and says, 'I'm sorry. The lady has to leave now.'

In prison you have to learn to grovel, because that's what they like. A lot of people say that they can do it their way, standing on their heads. That's not possible. No way. No chance. What you've gotta do is think about it and say, 'Right. Here I am. Shut the door. That's it.' Right now my eyes are bad, but when I've got glasses and I've got a book, I can forget about the outside world and just lie there. Being little, I have played on my size to get away with a lot. You can talk to one of the screws, feel their faces, and if you think he's got a bit of time for you, you get hold of him. 'I need a job,' you say, because that's the answer, keeping yourself occupied.

Wandsworth is the hardest nick in Britain. They give you a rough time. It's got so many wings and they're all closed in. You can't go out in the gardens. You can't move. D Wing is the heavy wing. That's where you get the lifers. Pentonville's easy. It used to be a hard nick, but you get all the dossers in there now doing seven days and fourteen days, and then they're out again. There's always plenty to drink in Pentonville. Years ago it used to have a topping-shed, and Wandsworth has still got one, even though they say they've abolished hanging. Well, they haven't, have they? You can still be topped for treason, arson in a naval dockyard or doing something naughty to the Queen, and that's why they've got a gallows down in Wandsworth. Last time I was in there, and it's not so long ago, I got myself a job as Number One tea boy, and my tea room was right next door to what we call the Mudie Library, where only the screws can go to get books. Once a month this door opens and through there go the magistrates, a Deputy or the Governor, and other people from the Home Office, and they test the apparatus to make sure it works. I've seen it myself; been in there and stood on the trap door where many poor buggers have spent their last moments alive. Everything is made of wood. The trap door is wood. There's a wooden beam over your head where they used to hang the rope, and a wooden lever at the side which they used to open the trap door; they would put the hood over your head, the noose around your neck with the knot under your ear, pull that lever, and down you'd go.

I was in Wandsworth the night they hung Derek

Bentley. That was a terrible thing. Bentley was innocent, really. He had already been arrested when that other feller, Craig, shot the policeman. We all knew Craig's brother, Peter, who was already doing bird, and we reckoned that Bentley had been led astray. Everyone thought it was very unfair and feelings ran high throughout the prison. People were shouting and screaming, and in the morning the screws locked us in our cells. I've been in prison a few times when people have been hung, but that was worse.

We all knew what was going on, and we knew where he was, 'cos they moved him into the death cell. He'd be sitting with his back to a door that he doesn't know is there, so that they can come in from behind and grab him by the arms before he knows what is happening. It's a comfy cell with its own private bathroom, and he can have a bath first if he wants to, and whatever he wants for breakfast, tea or coffee, or even a wee dram, but he doesn't actually know when his moment has come because it's quiet and they've taken his watch away, and no one's telling him the real time. Then that door opens very quietly and in comes the hangman together with the rabbi or the priest, or whatever, depending upon his religion, and they take him next door to the shed. That night we could hear hundreds of people outside in the street, shouting and protesting. It was a terrible night, and they brought us breakfast in our cells next morning in case things got out of hand. Had we all been together, there could have been a riot.

I was in Brixton for stabbing that geezer outside the London Palladium when Reggie and Ronnie were brought in, in January 1965. That was the first time the Old Bill tried to get them both, and they were accused of demanding money with menaces from the feller who had the Hideaway Club. They were put in adjoining cells and I was in the cell next door, so we could talk to each other, and I could get them whatever they needed. I'd been grovelling again, and had got myself the job that I wanted, Number One tea boy again. That meant the screws left my cell door open all the time so that I could fetch them their tea and coffee whenever they wanted it.

Well, that's easy, isn't it? You just lie there on your bed, reading a book, and then when they call you, you say, 'Right you are. In a minute,' and you pop across to the tea room, put the kettle on, and make them their cup of tea. If they want a T-bone steak or whatever, you pop that under the grill, chip some potatoes and throw them into the pan, and there's no questions asked, 'cos you've made life easier for them and they don't mind if you do a bit of business. They just turn a blind eye, plus, PLUS! Often they'll offer you a drink, and do little things for you, 'cos you're helping them. When Reggie and Ronnie were in the nick, I could get messages in and out, all the time, no problem. Some of the younger cons didn't like it. 'He's making the screws' tea, so he must be a grass,' they'd say, but they don't know the score. You've gotta grovel.

One time when I was in Pentonville, there was a woman working there who was coming up to retirement. I won't mention her name in case this gets her into trouble. Her mates had organised a collection among the screws, who all put in their ten pences. That raised fifteen quid, which wasn't enough for the stereo she wanted, so I says, 'How much have yer got?' When they tells me I says, 'Now don't say nothing, will yer?' and digs into the roll of notes I used to have in my waistband to chip in ten quid. She was amazed. 'I don't know how you do it,' she says, starting to cry, 'cos the screws haven't put in much and I've chipped in that cock and hen, tears rolling down her cheeks.

'Here, don't do that,' I says. 'Have a cup of tea.'

Anyway, wasn't my money, if you know what I mean. I'd been dealing again. I could sell that liquid cannabis in roll-ups at £5 a time, but I'd take a quid if that was all they'd got. The other gear, the strong cannabis, was going for £20, and ordinary tobacco was worth £10 an ounce. I'm always buying and selling, even tea bags if I've got'em, because that's the name of the game. Duck and dive, gotta survive.

On the day they let me out of the nick, I sat there in a queue waiting for the grant of fifty or sixty quid that they give you, and then walked out through the prison doors with nearly £400 strapped around my leg with elastoplast. I hadn't smoked any of that stuff myself. Give me whisky every time.

I don't think prison serves any purpose. Prison doesn't do anyone any good. It has hurt me. It's ruined my family, ruined a lot of things. I've done sentences of seven years, four years, three years, two years, eighteen months, twelve months, nine months, six months, four months, three months and Borstal, and all it's done has kept me out of the way for a while. I am not happy to think of all the bird I have done. I'm not proud. I would have hoped that I could have gone on the straight and narrow, but I've done it and that's it, and I can still say that I have never hurt an innocent person. When you're a villain, you never do that. You get your information, plan your job, and then do it nice and cool. No one gets hurt, and the only people who are out of pocket are the insurance companies. I can't stand these fucking muggers, hurting old ladies, and those buggers who attack little children. Now, they should be locked up – and I'd take 'em round the corner first and give 'em a whipping. And I don't blame the blacks. No way, 'cos whites do it, too. The real villains would never hurt an old lady; they'd rather give 'em a helping hand.

Chapter 12

No matter what I've done, there's always been Leicester Square to go back to. That's been home to me for forty years. Whenever I've travelled abroad, toured with a show, worked in pantomime or been sent away, I've always gone back there. My father taught me that you can always make a living on the Square, and everyone knows me.

All the dossers kept coming to see me when I was banged up in Pentonville once, to let me know that my daughter Karen was speeding. On the day they released me, I went straight down to the Square and found her with this pusher, Petal, who's a poofter. I slapped her, which is the only time I'd ever slapped her, put her in a taxi and told the driver to take her straight home to Stayner's Road, and then I done Petal over with my walking stick 'cos he'd been giving her the pills. When they're speeding, they mix 'em and don't know what day it is. They get carried away. Everything's high, but when they come off it there's bad music. She's all right now. I stopped that, and I've stopped my Simon coming up to the Square as well. He was starting to play the machines, so I've told him to stay at home 'cos there's too many boys in there selling their arses, and he's a good-looking boy.

You've gotta protect your kids, 'cos the Square's a dangerous place, but there's always money around, you can always make bread.

I never liked working in films or television, 'cos it takes up so much time. You have to be there day after day for rehearsals, and the directors leave you hanging about. That's why I prefer busking, street entertaining, 'cos I like to be free, to be able to do what I wanna do and not have to be at a studio at six o'clock in the morning.

I've had a great life, but when I was doing that heavy bird, that seven-year sentence, it hurt me and when I came out in 1976, having earned my remission, I saw everything different. That's why I am living here now [St Mungo's]; my Sylvia couldn't suffer the drink, and I can hardly blame her, and when you've been away so long everything's changed. By the time I came out, the Chinese had taken over. The Maltese and the Italians had mostly gone. With the Chinese it's gambling and drinking; they're not into prostitution at all, no way. They're good to me. They give me money or food if they see I'm down, and otherwise leave me alone.

When I was in show business we used to have what we call 'resting' periods, but I don't rest, and never have done. It's boring being at home all day so I go out busking. I've been doing it for years, all the time I had the barrows as well; must have been thirty years, or even more.

Back in the forties I used to work with Dorothy Squires' father. We called him 'Muttoneye'. He had one eyeball missing and never wore a glass one, and the socket was bloody. He used to come down to the old Queen's Hotel, right next door to the Warner Theatre, with a portable piano, and he'd sit there in a bowler hat, jacket and tails playing that old Joanna, and then I'd take the hat around, which is what we call 'bottling'. I'm a great bottler, one of the best.

In those days the bottlers always used a hat, but the trouble with that was the punters could always see how much you were getting. Then the banks came out with the cloth bags for carrying money, and that's what I use because they can drop their silver inside without seeing what's already in there. I started working with Muttoneye when I was 13 years old, 'cos he came from East Ham, too, top of Central Park. At the end of a night he would put his hand in the hat and give me a handful of money and that would be my pay. He would never count it, just give me the handful.

Even then when you were working a queue, the women were always the best. 'Give him something, give him something,' you can hear 'em saying to their fellers, and then you know you're gonna be OK. You can tell who's gonna drop something into the bag, after all the years I've been doing it.

In the old days, the Old Bill used to leave us alone. For five or six years they've been giving us a hard time, especially since there's been this pedestrian precinct around the top of the Square. There's all these skinheads and junkies, with the Old Bill moving them on all the time, but they've eased up a bit on us just lately since I complained to Scotland Yard that I was being persecuted. That was after I'd been done for obstruction, and had been told to turn up at Bow Street Magistrates Court.

When it was my turn to go into the witness box, I put my hand on my head and held the Bible.

'You're supposed to hold the Bible in your left hand,' they said.

'I'll hold it in whichever hand I like, and I'll swear to tell the truth, the whole truth and nothing but the truth,' I said, bomp. Then I said, 'Now, can I ask this officer a question?'

'Yes,' they said.

'Now, officer,' I said. 'How wide would you say that the pavement was outside the Odeon in Leicester Square? Would you reckon it's about 8ft?'

'Yes.'

'Was there a big queue?'

'Yes,' he says again.

'Was they standing three or four abreast?'

'I think so,' he says.

'Now take your time, officer,' I says. 'I was walking up and down the queue, right?'

'Yes.'

'So it was the queue that was causing the obstruction, wasn't it, officer? If I'm walking up and down and they're standing still, how can I be the one that's causing the obstruction?'

After that the magistrates said there was insufficient evidence, and let me go. 'Thank you very much,' I said, 'cos I'm always polite. Outside in the corridor this woman comes up to me and says, 'Excuse me, are you Royston?'

'Yes, madam,' I said, taking my hat off. I thought it was a bloody solicitor, or something.

'You won't remember me. I'm Margaret . . .'

'You're talking about Somerset, aren't you?' I said. 'Lady Constance Ryder and Lady Audrey Anson.'

'You've got it,' she says. It was Lady Margaret Coke, who was their niece. She and her sister Kathleen are both interpreters attached to the Bow Street, Vine Street and Marlborough Street courts. One lives in Regent's Park and the other lives in Kensington. 'We thought you were very cute,' she says. 'You were a good jockey, and we all used to watch you riding bareback.'

Another time the Old Bill stopped me in the Square for having a stolen radio, and I had to go all the way to Lewes, wearing handcuffs, before they let me go, and then not so long ago they stopped me and said I was carrying a stolen shoulder bag. That wasn't true, either. I'd bought it. If I see them coming when I'm working the queue outside the Leicester Square Odeon, I dive through the queue and run up the stairs where there's a bar, and you can look through the window to see if they've gone.

I'm out working the queue most nights, unless it's wet. The best money is made at Christmastime, especially if there's Walt Disney films being shown. I made a lot of money with the Peter Sellers *Pink Panther* films and that was at the Odeon again. That Odeon never fails me. I have done so many films. The important thing for me is that the distributors put the films out in the West End first, because then people come up to town to see them so that they can see the films while they're new and they've read about them in the papers. When the films are put out on general release, that kills it for me. They did that recently with *Crocodile Dundee II* and *Throw Mama off the Train*, which had both been pulling in the crowds.

When *Gandhi* was showing, I did well for three months, made fortunes. It was such a puller, and it was only being shown at the Odeon to start with, so we were happy. It was so busy that I brought in three one-man bands – Mark, Martin and Scotty – to work the queue with me every night so that we could all have a break. I worked it first to get the punters in a good mood, and then they'd come along behind me, one behind the other, until I'm up by the lamp-post at the top of the Square, when I'd go for a wee dram. When you're working a queue like that, you mark someone – say, a feller in a bowler hat – and start again when he's nearing the front. It was hard work, but we took between us £11,000 in three months. Mark was the accountant. Although he's a junkie, he's a good boy and will help anyone. He took the money down to the bank. Not to bank it! Good God, no! To change it all into notes.

Gandhi was wonderful. People were giving us fivers, and one day a feller gave me £50. I had gone to meet my daughter and had my ukelele with me. She was a bit late, so I was standing there outside the Beefeater, tinkling with the ukelele, and a dwarf Arab with another big Arab asks me to play. So away I goes:

> Any old iron, any old iron,
> Any, any, any old iron

and he puts his hand in his pocket, pulls his wallet out and bungs me a note.

'I can't take money off a little feller like him,' I says to the big Arab, and then he tells me that the little geezer's a millionaire. 'Ah well, that's different,' I says, thinking that he had given me a tenner. But it was a fifty. The first

£50 note that I had ever had in my hand. I still hadn't looked at it, but saw me daughter and gave her the tenner which I already had in me pocket and then went back to Scotty. 'Here, I've just copped a tenner,' I told him.

'Where?' he says.

'Here,' I says. 'Off a dwarf Arab,' and shows him the note.

'You silly sod,' he says. 'That's a fifty.'

So I put it behind the ramp, behind the bar in the pub, and the guy says, 'Cor. I didn't know you was a millionaire. I can't quite change it,' so I tells 'im to buy all the lads a drink, and we ended up doing thirty of it in the pub. Sweet. You don't miss it 'cos you got it for nothing.

'Are we going back to work tonight?' one of the one-man bands says.

'Nah,' I says. 'We'll give it a miss, and go back to work tomorrer.'

We had another good tickle at the BBC Theatre in Upper Regent Street when they were doing a programme called *Walt Disney's Sixty Years*. It was massive. We used to start at nine o'clock in the morning and work through until four o'clock in the afternoon, breaking now and then for a wee dram. The show only lasted a fortnight, but we made hundreds.

Really and truly, that show was a rip-off because the kids didn't have to pay to go in, but once they'd go inside with their parents there were all these Mickey Mouse T-shirts, books, cartoons, toys, magazines, posters, and all that crap, which seemed a right rip-off to me. It cost the people more than they would have had to pay for tickets, which was why I was glad I got 'em while they were still outside. If I'd been there while they were coming out, I'd have had nothing. That was every day bar Sunday for two weeks, but who wants to work Sundays? That's the day I go to church, praise the Lord and say, 'Thank you very much.'

Whenever I'm busking, I always stop when I've got enough. I feel the weight of my bag to see if there's enough for my medicine. If that's OK, it's bye-bye, baby. I'm off. I also pack up if I get tired, and when it's raining I always work the inside of the queue and push the punters out on to the pavement, and let them get wet. Then, when I've done the queue, I go to the commissionaire and say in a loud voice, 'Now I don't want all them people to get wet. Will you let them wait inside, please.' And if he does, out come their purses and their wallets. I've a lot of little tricks like that.

If I see the punters smoking, I say, 'Excuse me, sir. Please don't smoke. You can see what it's done for me. Stopped me growing. Now Snow White has sacked me and I'm out of work, and I'll never be a big boy now – give us a cigarette!' Then I takes his cigarette, has a couple of puffs and throws it away. That's when I know his missus will whisper, 'Give him something' – and I'll be all right.

You must always be polite when you work the queues 'cos you never know when they're gonna come back. Sometimes they might not have any money on them, but you must still take your hat off while you watch them fumbling in their pockets. If they haven't got it, you don't get it. It's like the old saying: never beg a beggar. That's what my father always used to tell me when we were out totting or working the knocker.

My ukelele must be thirty or forty years old. I bought her just around the corner. I had another one just like her, but this one was given to me by Babs, a striptease artiste who works with a python and plays a guitar. She is well into her forties now, but she's still a very good entertainer. A long, long time ago her husband was very naughty to her. She would go to work, and he'd just wait at home doing sod-all, taking her money when she came home, so she gave him the heave-ho. My Simon is into pythons as well, but hers is an eight-footer. You can't give 'em dead meat because a python wants the fur, so you have to hold a gerbil or a rabbit head first, and then let the python swallow it live. The python then takes two weeks to digest it. My Simon screamed when he saw me picking up one of his rabbits one day. 'What are you gonna do, Dad?' he said. But I said, 'You haven't been feeding her, have yer?' and yer have to be cruel to be kind. The python can smell the rabbit just like a dog, and the rabbit never cries; you can see the rabbit slithering down the python's belly, and then he curls up and has a little sleep.

Babs doesn't work the street any more, but she bottled for me about four months ago. I had fallen out with two of the lads so she said, 'Let me come and work with you tonight.'

'OK,' I says, telling her how to work the queue, to wait until I had hit them with the verbals or the harmonica, and then to move up the queue right behind me. 'Take your time and just watch me,' I told her, and then come in right behind me, holding out the bag, saying 'Thank you very much, sir' or 'Do you like the little man?'

When you are working the queues, you don't have to be a good musician. You only have to strum your ukelele or play a few bars on the harmonica. It's the verbals that count. I've had all these geezers down here with their guitars and amplifiers, taking about two hours to tune up, and I've sacked 'em all. While they're still farting about, I just whip out my harmonica and then it's –

> One for the money, two for the show.
> Three to get ready, and go cat go

Sometimes I hit them with just one note on the harmonica, and say, 'Can you name that tune in one?' and that's enough to get 'em laughing. Then I say, 'Now I'm gonna play a tune for Margaret Thatcher,' before playing a few bars of *Hang Down Your Head, Tom Dooley* and singing,

Hang down your head, Mrs Thatcher
Hang down your head and cry
Hang down your head, Mrs Thatcher
Little Legs is walking by

That's silly, but it gets 'em laughing, and that's half the battle, 'cos when they're happy they'll put their hands in their pockets.

To tell the truth I can't sing, can't play the ukelele, can't play me harmonica, but I've got bottle and I can get 'em going, and when the tourists are in the queues I can hold my own in German, Italian, Chinese and a little bit of French. Usually I do better on my own without a bottler. Babs is a good bottler, but so many of 'em don't know how to time it right, whereas I know when I'm giving 'em the fun and games whether I've got 'em or not. I can feel when the time is right to hit 'em in the pocket.

Freight train, Freight train,
Going so fast

and I'll whizz down that queue with my bag.

Other times I'll start behind the queue board, and say, 'Now, listen. I'm not going to do a lot tonight 'cos I'm poorly, but I'm gonna entertain you and make you laugh.' Then I'll go up to a geezer and tell him, 'Now you're a nice boy. Look at that dimple there!' and that gets 'em going. Then I turns to his lady and says, 'Well, pet. Has he been a good boy?' and if she says, 'Yes,' I gives him a nudge and that gets her started . . . and then I'll move up the queue a bit and say, 'I'm sorry. I'll have your money in a minute. Margaret Thatcher has told me I've gotta have me cold tea every fifteen minutes. That's union rules,' and then I stand in the doorway, take out a half-bottle of Teacher's, turn to the queue and says, 'Anyone want some cold tea?' with me hand over the last five letters. That gets 'em laughing again, and then out comes the ukelele or the harmonica.

You have to use your noddle and time the queues. I always start at the Odeon, move across the Square to the Warner and then the Empire, and then down to the Leicester Square Theatre, and I'll move on to the Haymarket if my bag's still light.

All the one-man bands have been down here. I worked with Don Partridge for a while, before and after he had his hits *Rosie, Blue Eyes* and *Breakfast on Pluto*. I used to bottle for him sometimes, but his trouble was that he was aggressive like me. It's the same old story. He sacked his manager and got greedy, and then one day he was late for the queue and I told him to 'Fuck off'. If people don't turn up on time, that's it. Finito.

There was another one-man band called Jimmy. He turned up one day with his guitar in his hand, a drum on his back and an amplifier, and he wanted to bottle for me. And all I had was my harmonica! 'Get the fuck,' I told him. 'You want to bottle for me when you've got all that gear? You're nothing but a fucking idiot!'

A lot of those one-man bands play the subways, but I don't like working 'em. Makes me feel claustrophobic, although I've done 'em now and again, when it's been raining. A few notes on the harmonica, and

> If I said I loved you
> Would you mind?

When it was raining I always used to do the umbrellas. There's good money in that. I had a girl called Alice, who came from East Acton, and I used to have her selling umbrellas down at the Tower of London. We fell out, but she was a good grafter. They cost me 99p a time and she could sell 'em for two-and-a-half or three. You ask for three quid if you think you'll get it. It's like selling cinema tickets, Cup Final tickets, Wimbledon, or whatever. You ask for what you think they'll pay, 'cos you can always come down a bit. I've always done very well at Wimbledon, but I came unstuck a year or two back at Twickenham. I hired a truck and took fifteen boys down from here (the St Mungo hostel) to stand in the queue for the England–Ireland game, which was bound to be a winner, but they couldn't get any tickets. That cost me everything I had at the time 'cos I had to give 'em all a good drink, and I ended up skint. I won't work there any more.

I've also done well with Christmas wrapping paper, and another time I was in Oxford Street and saw these Japanese water-flowers in Woolworth's. Straight away I tumbled something. I went in and bought one. You just pop 'em in a glass, and then they grow in water, but all they look like is little bits of paper. So I went out and bought all the raffia paper I could find, got two girls to help me cutting it up into little bits with sharp scissors, and then popped them into bags, and had four workers out in Oxford Street, selling 'Grow Your Own Japanese Water Flowers'. We made a lot of money with that con, but the Old Bill got me and I was fined eighty quid.

It's what my father said: There's money out there on the streets. I have never steadily worked at any one thing. It's always been a little bit of this and a little bit of that, and when I've been nicked for something it's only been for whatever I've been doing that day. Every day's been different.

What I've liked about the street, and the villains, is the friendship. I've got a lot of enemies, but a lot of friends. If anything happened to me, there's a lot of people that would go out looking for the feller who did it. I can be a very nice person. I like to be happy, I mean HAPPY, but I can't stand people taking the piss.

At one time I used to work with a guy we called Johnny Eagle. He was a chain man down at the Tower of London. He would tie himself up with chains and handcuffs and then I'd tie him in a sack, and while he was getting himself out I'd go round with the hat. He would then bottle for me while I did my act. I used to have a parakeet that was trained to sit on my shoulder, and I would stand on my head, do a spin, and then fall down flat out on a mattress, and the parakeet would fall down beside me as if it was dead.

When Johnny died, his brother Frank tried to take over, but we soon sorted him out. One day, he came down and tried to take over our pitch. This was when I was doing a spell up the Portobello Road with Martin, the one-man band. Martin had left his drum on the pavement, which is the sign we leave to say that this is our pitch, and we'd gone off to the pub. When we came back, there was Frank, tying himself up in his brother's chains.

'What do you think you're doing?' I said.

'What's it got to do with you?' he says.

'This is our pitch.'

Now, he was new and he didn't have what we call a rook, someone to work with and tie him up in his sack. Instead, he was asking the public to tie him up, so I waited until he was inside the bag, and then said to the guy who was doing it, 'Let me take over,' and then laid him on the ground and roped him up good and proper. Then I gave him a kick and said, 'Now you get out of that...' The crowd all burst out laughing because they thought it was part of the act. Martin started playing his one-man band, and I went round with the bag!

Chapter 13

Four years ago I was on my arse. I wasn't finished, but I was skint. That's how it's often been. Loaded one day, skint the next. It's been a good life, a wonderful life. I've made fortunes, and the Old Bill have only captured me *sometimes*. I've had three wives, including Heddy, who was a common law wife, which is much the same thing. I've been a playboy and a villain. Fucked 'em and lost 'em. Although I'm a dwarf, I could still pull birds and even now, at my age, I still pull 'em.

That old man river
That old man river
He just keeps rolling
He keeps on rolling
That old man river
He keeps on rolling along

There are other things I would like to have done with my life. I would love to have been a star, and made enough money to open a nice hotel, meeting people easier than I've been able to do on the street. I've had that couple of pubs, but that's not the same. In hotels you get to know people.

I've always enjoyed meeting people, and I've met lots of 'em in my life. Film stars, stage stars, pop stars, royalty, villains. I've met 'em all, and often felt sorry for 'em 'cos they haven't had the advantages I've had.

Last time I was in the nick for anything serious was in 1980. That was for deception. As soon as they saw me come in the door at Pentonville, I was back on the hot plate. In comes Jack Parnell, the Palladium band leader. He had been sent down for drunken driving in his Roller. Knocked a motor bike over. This kid had to have his leg amputated. The girl who was riding pillion was injured badly. It had obviously cost him a fortune 'cos his insurance wouldn't have covered him for that, and Jack had a guilty conscience. It was troubling him. He was an old man and I felt sorry for him. I put in a word for him so he could get a job in the library. That's an easy number. He died a few months later.

The same time another feller comes in called Hugh Cornwell. Said he was lead guitarist with a pop group called The Stranglers. He had been done for drugs offences.

'I'm Hugh Cornwell,' he says.

'Oh, yeah.'

'I'm with The Stranglers.'

'Big deal!' I gave him a bucket and a brush and told him to clean the floor. No mop. Just a scrubbing brush. And he did not like it. I tell you: HE DID NOT LIKE IT!

But they're all the same to me, people. No one's better than anyone else. Some of 'em used to say that I played on my size, and I would take it. They might even give me a slap, 'cos I'm little, and I'd take that, too – but they'd never be able to take what they had coming to them. Even now that I'm getting old in years I can still take care of myself. I'm a loner. When I go down Leicester Square of an evening I don't need minders. I don't need bodyguards. I just do my own thing, playing the queues. If I miss, I miss. You win some, you lose some. I never mind 'cos I'm a loner. I like company, but when I'm out on that street I'm a loner, on my own, don't need no one. Sometimes women try to dictate to me. 'You can't do this' or 'You can't do that,' and then it's 'Bye-bye, baby, bye-bye' – I'm down the road.

The last one tried to get me off the drink. A lot of people have tried that, but the drink is me. I don't go after the bottle. The bottle finds me. It's like a magnet. When I go walking down that street, it comes out of the off-licence door and follows me down the road.

Whisky relaxes me. In the mornings I often wake up with the shakes, but then I vomit and bring up the bile, and I'm all right again once I've had another whisky. The whisky makes me lisp, which is unfortunate, but I can still go out and work. I drink two bottles a day and in the end it will kill me. The liver and kidneys give me pain now. Some days I'm doubled up with pain on me bed and can't move, and me knees are bad with arthritis. I keep falling over, but I've never been drunk in me life.

One day I was walking down Regent Street to do a bit of business and didn't have me walking stick with me, which was silly 'cos that left knee gives me trouble. I was going to work a queue, and fell arse over hip and landed on me tummy. This special constable comes up and picks me up.

'Thank you, officer,' I said, rubbing my knee.

'Are you drunk?' he says.

'No,' I says, but he tells me to walk down a white line in the road and when I fell over again he nicked me. Then he called a van and had me taken to Vine Street.

'I didn't want to do it,' he says, 'but it's for your own sake,' and when I appear before the magistrates next morning he puts in a good word for me, says he thinks I'd had an accident. They fine me £5 or a day's imprisonment, which means you're free to go without paying the fine because staying overnight in the cells counts as a day's imprisonment.

'Thank you very much ,' I says, and waits outside the court for him to come out, 'cos I thought I'd take him for a drink, but he wouldn't have one 'cos he was teetotal. That's the only time I've been done for drink, but they still pull me in now and then for minor things like obstruction, although some of 'em are a bit chary when they see me coming down the street.

Only the other night this copper came along and said, 'Would you mind moving along, please?'

'Yer what?' I says.

'You're pestering the queue,' she says.

'I'm what? They love me!'

'But you're begging,' she says.

'You're joking,' I says, because I had me ukelele strung across me chest and the money bag in me hand. 'You're gonna do me for begging, pet?' I says. 'You'll lose it!' And the queue was loving it, and I'm still walking through 'em with me money bag.

'Are you gonna nick me now?' I says, as we reach the end of the queue.

'Not if you go away.'

'I'll go away now,' I says, and goes around the corner to the next queue. There's a sergeant there, standing with another of the Old Bill, and this woman constable comes up and says to me, in front of them, 'You embarrassed me in front of all those people.'

'I embarrassed you? I think you were in the wrong,' I says.

'You're horrible,' she says.

'We've known Royston for a long time,' says the sergeant. 'He's no trouble . . .'

I've always lived off my wits. I wouldn't say I've made a good living, but I've survived and that's what you've gotta do. Duck and dive. Supposing you had never got me this bottle of whisky [which he was then drinking], I'd have had a wee dram here and a wee dram there, and if this one hadn't come along I can guarantee you that I would have gone out on that street and got another one. That's the wits. Survival.

It's like when my daughter was run over when she was 19, and I went in to see her at the Royal Free Hospital in Hampstead. She was on traction. If it had been a guy that had done it, I would have killed him but it was a woman, driving a green Cortina. The police and the nurses are all there, and I'm freaking out, 'cos she's my daughter and she's small like me, and there she is, lying in bleeding traction. The doctor says she'll be in fifteen weeks, right over Christmas, and I'm welcome to stay with her.

'Now look, it's Christmas Day, pet,' I says to her, and I'd got no money. I left there and walked back to Covent Garden, and by the time I'd reached Tottenham Court Road tube station I'd made thirty-seven quid. I'd blagged 'em all, not the way these silly winos do, but the right way, raising my hat and saying, 'Merry Christmas, sir,' as I passes 'em all in the street.

'How are you?' they say.

'Well, I would be happy,' I says. 'My daughter has got run over and she's having to spend Christmas in the Royal Free', and that's when they say, 'Can we give her a present?' THIRTY-SEVEN QUID!

How much money do you think I spend a week on whisky? It's gotta be a long 'un (£100). Easy, EASY. Twenty-five years ago I was in hospital, and we're talking about East Ham again – the Memorial Hospital, East Ham – and the doctor says to me, 'Your liver's frozen, and your kidney, that one (touching my side) is naughty.' He advises me to give up the whisky there and then.

'Yeah, I'll think about it,' I says.

'If you don't lay off it, you won't be here too long,' he says – and that was twenty-five years ago.

Last time I was in hospital was three or four years ago. That was an ulcer then, and I should be back in there now because I'm having trouble with my bowels. I had haemorrhoids and they cut 'em, but they didn't do a good job and I need to go back in again. People don't believe this, but it's the whisky that helps me through. They think it does your brain in, but for me it's a cure. I have to have my first half-bottle before I can start the day. I don't take pills or drugs of any sort, so my only cure is this.

Four years ago I was sleeping on the Embankment, underneath the Arches. Flat on my arse. Skint, but still pulling in enough every day from the queues to buy me a wee dram. I'd been in the nick and couldn't go back home.

My wife couldn't suffer the drink, and I don't blame her for that, so that's where I went. Two mates of mine looked after me sleeping bag during the day, and then I'd go off busking the queues and come back with a carrier, with a bottle of Martini for one of 'em, cider for the other, bottle of Scotch for me, and some fags to see us through the night. One night I finish the queues, go down the Tom Cribb for a wee dram, and then catches a taxi down to the Apollo, which is the supermarket just by the Arches.

'Where do you live, sir?' says the driver.

'There,' I says, pointing to me sleeping bag on the pavement.

'Oh, the flat,' he says, thinking I have the flat over the fish 'n' chip shop.

'No,' I says, pointing again, and telling him that that sleeping bag was mine and that the fellers were looking after it for me during the day, and that I'd brought 'em back their supper. He doesn't tell me, but the driver goes straight back to Leicester Square and tells my mate, Scotty, where I'm sleeping. Scotty comes down in a taxi, and takes me straight round to St Mungo's. After I'd been there a few months they chucked me out for fighting. That was just after Christmas 1983, and it was a good Christmas, but I gave this feller a spank. Then I came back here again in January 1986 and they gave me a room of my own.

There's many people around here far worse off than me. You gotta feel sorry for 'em. I was standing on the platform at Tottenham Court Road tube station the other day, and saw this geezer looking at two girls. As their train comes, he whips out his cock and starts masturbating so's they can see him through the window as the train leaves the station. And people think I've got problems! There's fellers in here (the St Mungo hostel) that I feel sorry for as well. Really, they shouldn't be here. They need medical or psychiatric attention, but the government is kicking 'em all out of the hospitals and there's nowhere else for 'em to go. A lot of 'em pee in the sink, but unfortunately I can't reach the sink – so I have to go walkies. That's where I meet Peter, who cleans the toilets here. I give him a bob or two and he cleans my room for me, and there's another feller, Robert, who does all my washing for me.

'We don't know how you do it,' they say when they see me walking around here with a bottle of whisky in me pocket, but it suits me, and I'm just around the corner from Leicester Square.

I don't eat much. I never have breakfast, but there's always this bile to bring up every morning. Sometimes I have a drop of milk first just to get the bile going, 'cos I've had a stone in my kidneys for twenty years. It'll be the kidneys or the liver that kill me, if the ticker doesn't go first; some days I'm in a lot of pain. Usually, I don't eat at all during the day and then I'll have something small like a toasted cheese sandwich or some vegetables. I like a bit of pickle or a gherkin, and some days I go down to the fish shop in Endell Street and have a bit of skate or a fillet of plaice. I'm not a lover of cod or haddock. I like a trout, but I can't afford 'em. I like to cook 'em myself, 'cos I don't like any oil, margarine or butter; just lay them in the oven and let them bake a little bit, and then souse them with vinegar.

Downstairs they have all this stuff from Marks & Spencer, food that hasn't been sold at the end of the day which they bring round here in crates, but I don't go much for that. You only pay £1 for your evening meal and 20p for a sweet. A cup of tea costs 12p, but you can only get one between 12 and 2 p.m. and then from 5 to 6 p.m., and then there's supper from 7 to 9 p.m. Whenever I go down there, I always check the sell-by dates because Marks & Spencer wouldn't be sending it down here if they could sell it, would they?

I don't sleep much, either. Don't forget my age. I'm 57 and I was taught you only need four hours' sleep at my age. What I do is twist and turn in bed, thinking about memories, and if I get four hours, that's enough. Often I don't get back here until 3 or 4 in the morning. It's all according to what I've been doing. I go down to Leicester Square in the evenings, work the queues, and then I'm usually finished by 9 p.m., and then I go off to the club. I only use two clubs, the Tin Pan Alley Club in Denmark Street, and another one down near Leicester Square that's a gay club upstairs with another bar downstairs where all the chaps go, the villains. I still see a lot of 'em about, and you'd be surprised how many of the younger boys come to me for advice.

If the weather's good during the day, I'll sit outside in the street, have a wee shant, and think about things. Sometimes I love to be on my own, just relaxed, because it's not easy working the queues. People think, 'Busker, money for nothing', but it's hard. You've gotta work for it.

Every few months I get a letter from the Job Centre asking me to turn up for an interview. I always tell 'em the same thing, 'If you can get me a job painting skirting boards, I'll bring me own ladder.' They always apologise for calling me, but I still get another letter next time.

As long as there's cash in my pocket, I'm happy. I haven't had a cheque book in twenty-five years, and it's no good me having a Barclaycard or an Access card 'cos I can't reach the machines. So it's cash all the time, which is the way it always was, in the theatre, wrestling or working the street. I like cash. It never bounces. The most cash I've ever had on me was eight grand (£8,000), but that was a good few years ago. When you've got money like that, you've gotta hide it, under the cushions, under the bed, on top of the wardrobe – or just bury it. I've still got my gypsy caravan down in South Benfleet, where I bought meself seven and a half acres of land years ago, when I had a bit of spare money. I've still got the land, but I let me brother Harry have two and a half acres to build a bungalow and he looks after the caravan for me. It's there, that's the thing, and if I have to go travelling again I know where to start. You never lose that if you're a gypsy.

Survival. That's the name of the game. If you're gonna survive, you've gotta go out on that street, 'cos that's where it is. I can make money. Even now. I've made bloody fortunes. Gor blimey, babes, have I enjoyed life! Please God – well I don't say God, say Karma, 'cos I don't believe in any other kind of religion, although I'm a Jew – if I die tomorrow, I can say I've had the best survival ever. I have had the greatest. The truth is in the pudding. I have made many mistakes: many, many, many – but I have no regrets, 'cos I've never hurt an innocent person. And that was my father's approach to life, too. That's where I got it from.

There's times when I'm lonely, 'cos a lot of my friends, and they're very good friends, have been locked away. Ronnie and Reggie are both inside, and they've got another ten years to do. Tony Knightley, Johnny Knight and Chico Davies are all doing eighteen, and Chopper Knight, who is one of the best friends I've ever had, is in there for thirty-three years, and I thank the Lord that I wasn't born as tall as them, because if I had I would be doing thirty years as well, or I'd be brown bread, 'cos I've always been game. All of 'em knew I was game, but they'd say, 'Sorry. We can't take you out on this one 'cos you're a dot on the card.' That's what they told me, every time.

Every couple of months my Karen gets a VO (a Visiting Order) from Ronnie to go down and see him in Broadmoor. He thinks the world of her, always has done, and says he'd like me to go down and see him as well, but he knows I can't handle it. He knows I still think of 'em as friends, and when they come out I'll want to see 'em. Until she died, I used to go round to see their Mum when she was running the Blue Coat pub near Liverpool Street station, and went to the party she had there when

Charlie came out, but I can't handle going to funerals, hospitals and seeing people in prison. I get too emotional. Ronnie gets very depressed 'cos he thinks he will never come out. Reggie can take more punishment. He's mentally strong, and can handle it, but thirty years is a hell of a time. They've got no Mum and Dad to come home to. All their family has gone, and I miss 'em all 'cos they were all bloody good to me.

Reggie and Ronnie have both sent me VOs, but they understand. I don't go to funerals, either. I didn't even go to my Mum's. It's like a superstition, only it's deeper than that, 'cos I keep remembering when I was banged up in the nick and I couldn't bear to see anyone, 'cos it was fucking my mind up. When my family came, I couldn't find words to speak and all I could say was, 'Go, please go!' When you've done a lot of bird, like I have, you know what it's like. If I went to see them I wouldn't be able to stop thinking about them doing thirty years and I'd get all choked up. So Karen takes the messages for me, and they understand. There's friendship between villains. You trust each other. You've got to. It's the best sort of trust I know.

Glossary

Roy Smith's everyday conversation is peppered by colourful slang phrases. Most are traditional East End words or phrases, including much rhyming slang, but there are also others that he has acquired during his years in the theatre, circus, wrestling, street trading, busking, as an active criminal, and in prison. Some are of ancient origin. The word 'punk' even appears in Shakespeare's plays. Others are more recent, coming from the United States since the sixties with the growth of drug-taking.

ACE, AN	£1
ALKY	alcoholic
APPLES	stairs (abb. for apples and pears in rhyming slang)
AUNT MARIA	fire
BAKER'S DOZEN	thirteen, the additional loaf being traditionally the street trader's profit
BANANA	tube used for snorting cocaine
BEES	money (abb. for bees and honey)
BEHIND THE RAMP	someone in authority; prison officers; housing officers; policemen behind a reception desk – the ramp is the obstacle between them and the citizen
BIN	pocket, often the waistcoat pocket
BIRD	term of imprisonment
BIT OF STICK	£5
BLAG	theft or burglary
BLAST	a telephone call
BLISTER	sister
BLOW, TO	to lose
BLOWER	telephone
BLOW-JOB	oral sex
BOAT RACE	face
BOTTLE	nerve or courage; the word can also mean £2 (i.e. 'a bottle')

BRACE, ON THE	on the roof; a term used when criminals are discussing, say, a burglary that necessitated going on to the roof of a building
BRASS, A	a prostitute
BRIEF, A	a solicitor or barrister
BROWN BREAD	dead
BUCK	someone employed to work on a fruit barrow on a freelance basis while the owner has time off
BUSYBODIES	police
CAP	being treated to drugs when you have no money
CAPTURED	arrested
CARPET	three months' imprisonment; can also mean £3 or £30
CASER	five shillings (a pre-decimal phrase that is now largely out of use)
CLARET	blood
COBBLES, as in ON THE COBBLES	ready for a fight
COCK AND HEN	£10
COW'S CALF	£150 (i.e. one and a half)
CORNER, THE	confidence trickery; the con-game
CREEP	thief
DABS	finger-prints
DANDRUFF	head-butt to the forehead, as in 'give him a dandruff'
DARBIES	handcuffs
DIP	pick-pocket
DIVE-BOMBER	a down-and-out who goes round the streets picking up cigarette dog-ends
DOG	telephone (abb. for dog and bone)
DOT ON THE CARD	someone well known, often meaning that he/she is too well known in criminal terms
DROPSY	bribery
DUCK AND DIVE, or DUCKING AND DIVING	the criminal way of life; rhyming slang for survive or surviving
DUMMY	wallet

DYNAMITERS	drug-pushers
FEEL FINE	£9
FINGER, TO	to grass or inform
FORK	hand
FROG	road (abb. for frog and toad in rhyming slang)
GAFF	home
GARDEN	£8
GEE-GEE	£1,000
GEEZER	person, usually male
GHOSTING OUT	when the prison authorities suddenly move a prisoner from one gaol to another, often because they suspect that he/she is up to some chicanery or planning to escape
GLASGOW KISS	head-butt to the nose
GOLDEN GATE	£800
GRAIS	caravans
GRASS	an informer, or informing (the word is used both as a noun and as a verb)
GROIN	a ring
HACK	a minder
HALF A BAR	ten shillings (a word dating back to pre-decimal currency days, and now used less frequently)
HAM	home (abb. for ham and bone)
HANDKERCHIEF, as in 'gave him the handkerchief'	to give one a signal, deriving from the common practice among criminals of making prearranged signs to each other in crowded places by the use of a handkerchief
HIKE	to take someone for a walk, usually meaning that the person concerned is going to be assaulted or even killed
HOISTING	shop-lifting
HOOK	crook
ICE CREAMS	punters or mugs who are potentially customers for prostitutes, street traders, pick-pockets, spivs or con-men
IRISH WHIP IN THREE	a wrestling phrase used when two wrest-

	lers have agreed that one of them will take a fall in the third round, often by an Irish whip which is single-handed left arm whip
JACK	a till (abb. for Jack and Jill)
JACK'S ALIVE	£5 usually, but sometimes £50
JAM-JAR	car
KETTLE	watch
KIP	sleep
KIPPER	hostel or boarding house
KITE	cheque
LAG	convict
LEGS ELEVEN	£11
LLOYD	a piece of celluloid or plastic used by thieves to open Yale and other locks
LOAF	head (i.e. loaf of bread)
LONG 'UN	£100
MACE or MACING	confidence trickery
MANOR	the area within which a criminal 'firm' operates; the word has now crossed the language barrier and is often used by the police as well to describe their own districts
MESSAGE	the euphemism for instructions given by one criminal to another suggesting that a third party be wounded or even killed, as in 'give Johnny the message'
MIKE MALONE	phone
MONKEY	£500
MONKEY-CLIMB	technique derived from wrestling where an assailant can attack a much larger man by jumping on his knee-caps and then delivering a head-butt
MOON	one month's imprisonment
MOTHER'S LIFE	imprisonment for life
MOUSE	an informer
MUG	a wally or idiot
NARK or NOAH'S ARK	an informer
NEEDLE, as in 'get the needle'	rage or anger

NEVIS	£7
NICK	police station
NICKED	arrested
NICKER	£1 (now less common)
NORTH AND SOUTH	mouth
NOUGHTS AND CROSSES	a criss-cross slashing with a razor, sometimes to the face, but more often to the buttocks
NOVICE	rotten apples (a phrase used between street traders when describing the condition of their fruit without customers being able to understand)
OLD BILL	police
ON THE CUFF	getting something without paying for it
ONCER	£1
ONE-AND-A-HALF	£150
PEN AND INK	drink
PETER	safe
PONCE	someone who arranges clients for prostitutes, protects them, or lives off their earnings
PONTOON	21 months' imprisonment
PONY	£25
PORCUPINES	lies (probably a corruption of pork pies in rhyming slang)
PORRIDGE	imprisonment
PUNK	a wally, a mug or an idiot – seldom used to describe skinheads!
PUNTER	a customer for a prostitute, street trader, spiv or clip joint
PUSH	when a robber knocks someone down, as in 'well, I gave him a push'
ROAF	£4 and sometimes £40 (probably deriving from the racecourse trick of spelling words backwards; it is similar to four spelt thus, but pronounced roaf as in loaf)
ROOSTER	someone who keeps a look-out while other criminals are committing a burglary or similar offence
RUCK	dispute

SCARPER	run away
SCRANNY	food, usually used to describe restaurant meals
SCREW (verb)	to rob
SCREWS	prison officers
SHANT	to have a drink, especially Scotch
SHAVE	to attack someone with a razor, as in 'gave him a shave'
SHOOTING GALLERY	this has two meanings – (i) drug addicts use it to describe places where drugs are available, and (ii) villains to describe venues for burglary, robbery or other crimes
SKINT	penniless
SMOTHER	overcoat
SNAKES	the term used when two wrestlers agree to take a fall so that the fight becomes even before the final round, thus spinning out the bout
SNIDE	fake jewellery or counterfeit coins or notes
SNOUT	tobacco
SPEEDBALL	a drug cocktail, usually containing both Valium and marijuana
SPIELERS	illegal gambling clubs
SPIVS	street traders or dealers who live by their wits
STAMP	post office
STEAMER	homosexual; other words used like gay, poof, poofter or queen already have much wider use
STICK	jemmy
STRETCH	12 months' imprisonment
STRIDES	trousers; another word that is now widely used
STRIFE	life sentence
STRIPE	a razor slash, usually to the face
SWEET AS A NUT	a transaction that went well
TANK	bank
TAPPING	begging
TEA	marijuana or cannabis

TEA-LEAF	thief
TEA-LEAVING	thieving
TICKLE	a criminal opportunity, often used when it has been successfully taken
TOPPED	executed by hanging
TOSHEROON	half-a-crown (2s 6d in pre-decimal currency; a word thus used less frequently, although common until the sixties)
TRICK OF TRIP	a prostitute's customer; originally the word trick was used, but trip has since become a derivation
TUB	£100
TURTLES	gloves (abb. for turtle doves)
TWEEDLE	a deception, often involving the substitution of phoney items like rings or jewellery for the real thing
TWIRLS	keys
TWO-ER	£200
UNCLE NED	bed
UNLUCKY FOR SOME	£13
UP THE FAIRGROUND	going to be lucky
UP THE STEPS	being sent for trial; likewise, down the steps signifies acquittal or immediate release without imprisonment, believed to be a reference to the steps of the Old Bailey
VERA LYNN	gin
VIPER	a euphemism for snake-bite, an injection of morphine and heroin
WALKING THE PONY, OF TAKING THE PONY FOR A WALK	going to the lavatory (rhyming slang for pony and trap, having a crap)
WET ON THE FRONT	phrase used by street traders to suggest that their fruit, particularly strawberries or cherries, are sweating and need to be sold quickly before their condition deteriorates
WHISTLE	suit (abb. for whistle and flute in rhyming slang)

Chronology

This chronology has been compiled to help readers place the events described in this book in a time-frame. Where possible, I have checked the dates against *The Times Index* in the Westminster City Reference Library, and also against their microfiches of *The Stage*. Dates have also been cross-checked against the books *The Profession of Violence: The Rise and Fall of the Kray Twins* by John Pearson, Weidenfeld & Nicolson (1972), and the revised edition, Grafton Books (1985); *Me and My Brothers* by Charles Kray with Robin McGibbon, Grafton Books (1988); *Our Story* by Reg and Ron Kray with Fred Dinenage, Sidgwick & Jackson (1988), *Murder Without Conviction* by John Dickson, Sidgwick & Jackson (1986), and *The Encyclopaedia of Murder* by Colin Wilson and Patricia Pitman, Arthur Barker (1961) and Pan Books (1984).

1931

30 October	Royston James Smith born deaf and dumb at 50 Wallace Road, West Ham, fifth of the seven children of Helen and Harry Granville Smith. His mother came from a Jewish family who had changed their name by deed poll from Marks to Paisley.

1933

24 October	Reggie and Ronnie Kray born in Bethnal Green, twin sons of Violet and Charlie Kray. Their mother also came from a Jewish family.

1938

	At the age of 7, Roy is injured in an accident with his mother's sewing machine and gains the powers of speech and hearing.

1939

25 June	Death of the gypsy John Loveridge on a gypsy camp site at Hartlebury Common near Bromsgrove, Worcestershire. During the commotion, Roy's mother tells him to come inside the family caravan and keep out of trouble.
18 October	Gypsy brothers William Smith (22) and Wisdom Smith (18) found guilty of manslaughter, and sentenced to ten years' penal servitude and five years' penal servitude, respectively.

1940–3

During the London blitz Roy is evacuated with his brothers and sisters to Knowle, a large mansion at Timberscombe, Somerset, where they are looked after by Lady Constance Ryder JP and her sister Lady Audrey Anson, daughters of the 4th Earl of Harrowby. The children return to London when their mother inherits a house in Strone Road, Manor Park, from their Aunt Nell; there was little risk of bombing there.

1944

December	Roy makes his stage debut as Bonzo the dog in the Richmond Theatre production of *Babes in the Wood* at Richmond, Surrey.

1945

Roy sent back to Somerset to attend an approved school at Blue Anchor, having nearly killed a boy at Timberscombe; his parents appeal on his behalf and are able to secure his return home to Strone Road after three months.

December	Roy again plays Bonzo the dog, this time in *Babes in the Wood* at the Palace Theatre, Watford.

1946

Roy and his family take to the road again in their caravan and trailer, first visiting Ickenham, Middlesex; then crossing London to stay in Kent, before taking off for the West Country.

1947

January–April — Roy returns to Timberscombe, renting a country cottage, and staying at village pubs around Exmoor, before rejoining his family.

21 December — Body of retired engineer William Bissett (71) found in a brook at Wraysbury near Slough, near a gypsy camp site. He had been missing three days and his suit was found hidden nearby in a drainpipe. It was later established that he had been talking to a gypsy at the Cock inn, and had been observed taking out a large bundle of notes from his pocket to buy drinks. Later a gypsy, Joe Smith (23), is charged with his murder . . . and Roy Smith vanishes.

1948

3 March — Joe Smith sentenced to death at Kingston Assizes. Court told that Bissett died as a result of violent blows with a fist. Other gypsies are said to have been involved, but remain untraced. Smith tells the court: 'When you sentence me to death you sentence an innocent man.'

6 April — Joe Smith's appeal dismissed in the Court of Criminal Appeal.

14 April — The House of Commons votes to suspend the death penalty for a trial period of five years.

17 April — The Home Secretary announces a reprieve for Joe Smith.

22 July — The House of Lords rejects the Commons' clause suspending the death penalty, with the effect that the penalty is restored.

By now Roy Smith is in the United States, having travelled there on the *Queen Elizabeth*. He tours the United States as a midget wrestler, but the tour comes to an abrupt end in Mobile, Alabama, when one of the wrestlers murders another in a dispute over a woman.

1949

Roy Smith spends nine months in Brixton Prison accused of burglary and breaking and entering. By now he is living in a one-room flat at St Stephens Gardens, Paddington.

December — Roy Smith opens in the pantomime *Babes in the Wood* at the Aston Hippodrome, Birmingham, appearing with Alfred Marks, Kathleen Moody and Paddy O'Neal.

1950

Roy meets the Kray brothers for the first time at the Joe Abrahams' gymnasium in Mile End, Bow. He drives over there daily from Paddington to practise weight-lifting; Reggie and Ronnie are both keen young boxers.

December — Roy opens in pantomime at the Alexandra Theatre, Birmingham, appearing in *Sleeping Beauty*.

1951

December — Roy opens in pantomime at the Birmingham Hippodrome, appearing in *Cinderella* with Arthur Askey and Arthur Haynes.

1952

March — Reggie and Ronnie Kray called up to do their National Service. They join the Royal Fusiliers, and are eventually court-martialled for striking an officer, going absent without leave, and 'conduct prejudicial to good order and discipline'. They spend nine months in military prisons at Colchester and Shepton Mallet, where Roy Smith visits them.

Roy Smith sent to prison for three years for stabbing a bookmaker's runner on Stepney Green.

2 November — Murder of PC Miles by Christopher Craig, and Derek Bentley. Bentley had already been arrested before Craig shot Miles, but Craig cannot be sentenced to death because he was only 16 years old.

1953

28 January — Derek Bentley executed at Wandsworth Prison, despite widespread public protests and petitions for mercy. Roy Smith is in the prison on the day of the execution, and is released a fortnight later.

18 February — The birth of Roy's first son.

15 July — Execution of John Reginald Halliday Christie for the Notting Hill murders.

December — Roy appears in the pantomime *Babes in the Wood* at the Swansea Grand with Stan Stennett and Ossie Morris, and later becomes part of Stennett's stage act, working as his 'feed' in variety tours on the Moss Empires and Stoll Theatres circuit.

1954

June — Roy leaves for the United States, knowing that his father is dying. For nearly four years he tours with the King Brothers and also the Ringland Brothers, Barnum and Bailey circuses, touring twenty-eight States. During this period he also appears in the film *Trapeze* with

Burt Lancaster; meets Marlon Brando, while Brando is filming *The Wild Ones*, and also appears in the film *The Greatest Show on Earth*.

18 June — Roy's father Harry Granville Smith dies of lung cancer, aged 63.

On being dishonourably discharged from the army, Reggie and Ronnie Kray take over the Regal billiard hall in Eric Street, Mile End, which soon becomes a central meeting point for East End villains.

1956

5 November — Ronnie Kray sentenced to three years' imprisonment at the Old Bailey for causing grievous bodily harm.

1957

Reggie Kray opens the Double R Club in Bow Road, Bethnal Green, and then later another club in Wellington Road. The Double R begins to attract show business celebrities; the other one becomes a centre for illegal gambling and bookmaking.

Winter — Roy Smith returns from the United States, having been deported.

1958

20 February — Ronnie Kray sent to Long Grove mental hospital near Epsom, Surrey, having been strapped in a strait-jacket and certified insane; he had been greatly distressed by the death of his Aunt Rose, and was later diagnosed as schizophrenic.

1959

Roy Smith works for nine months with the Morton Fraser Harmonica Gang, touring in variety.

December — After a dispute with Morton Fraser, Roy Smith joins the *Snow White and the Seven Dwarfs* ice show at the Wembley Empire Pool. He spends sixteen months with the company, touring Glasgow, Bristol, Newcastle, Birmingham, Manchester and Liverpool; appearing in summer season at Brighton, and then returning to Wembley for a second season there in December 1960. During the Liverpool season, Roy Smith is presented to the Queen and the Duke of Edinburgh at a Royal Command Performance of the show.

1960

19 May — Questions asked in Parliament about growing gang warfare and protection rackets in London. Marcus Lipton MP says: 'The club problem has become an outrageous scandal ... a breeding ground of corruption.'

Reggie Kray sent to prison for eighteen months after being linked with a 'Chicago-style protection racket'.

June — Roy's mother Helen Smith dies while he is appearing in the *Snow White and the Seven Dwarfs* summer show in Brighton. While appearing there he meets Patricia Lendrum, then a dancer, whom he later marries.

Autumn — The Krays take over Esmeralda's Barn, a gaming club in Wilton Place, Belgravia, which gives them an estimated income of £40,000 per annum (according to Pearson's *The Profession of Violence*). Lord Effingham later joins their board of directors.

1961

May — The police fail in their first attempt to nail the Krays. Reggie is found Not Guilty of housebreaking when a woman witness fails to identify him in the dock at his appearance before East London Magistrates. Ronnie and Charlie are both found Not Guilty of 'loitering with intent to commit a felony'. They call a press conference at Esmeralda's Barn to claim that they are being victimised.

Roy Smith joins The Three Monarchs, a harmonica trio working in variety and on television. He works with them for nearly a year.

July — Reggie and Ronnie Kray become associated with various East End charities. They are photographed with the Mayor of Bethnal Green, Councillor Hare, at the St Matthews Youth Club dance, helping to raise funds for the church organ. They also help to raise funds for old age pensioners, youth clubs, boxing clubs and local hospitals.

Ronnie moves into Cedra Court, Walthamstow, and begins building up the 'firm', employing villains in various West End establishments where Reggie has arranged for the payment of protection money.

1962

March — Princess Margaret and Lord Snowdon attend the premiere of the film musical *Sparrers Can't Sing* at the Empire Cinema, Bow Road. Afterwards many of the cast and other celebrities attend the celebration party at the Krays' newly opened Kentucky Club, just across the road. Roy Smith is among them.

Roy Smith starts operating his fruit stall in Argyll Street, outside the London Palladium, having had fruit stalls in Soho since the late forties.

April — Jet Harris leaves Cliff Richard and The Shadows after the incident at the Marlborough

Head, when Roy Smith gave him a hiding; Harris went on to begin a solo career with Tony Meehan, which eventually collapsed.

Roy Smith opens the Midgets Club in Gerrard Street, Soho, and then later the same year opens the Kismet Club in Great Newport Street, with his brother Raymond 'fronting'.

6 November — Roy Smith marries Patricia Lendrum at Caxton Hall register office. They had met while he was appearing in *Snow White and the Seven Dwarfs*, and later she became a hostess at the Latin Quarter night club. That evening they held a party at the Kismet Club.

12 December — Roy Smith put on probation for two years at the London Sessions after telling the court that he had committed burglaries in Hertford Street, Mayfair, and in Stoke Newington to pay for his wedding. He had been on remand in Brixton Prison for thirty-five days, and the case made headlines in every national newspaper.

That year alone the Krays are thought to have made over £100,000 just through their long-firm frauds – buying goods through companies that quickly went bankrupt after the goods had been sold off. (*Source:* Pearson's *The Profession of Violence*.)

1963

3 February — Reported in *The Sunday People* that the police are hunting for two gangs 'who have moved into the Soho protection racket'. This was the first press reference to the activities of the Kray and Richardson gangs.

Roy goes into the secondhand car business, taking a site in Roman Road, Bethnal Green,

1 April — Roy Smith makes his first midget wrestling appearance in Britain at Bedford Alhambra,

and later goes on to promote midget wrestling throughout Britain, with the dwarf Tommy Gallagher as his partner in the ring.

21 April — *The Sunday People* begins serialising Roy Smith's life story, with subsequent episodes appearing on 28 April and 5 May – the story was far from truthful with Smith making no references to the Krays, and saying of his December court appearance that it was 'the first time the Law had managed to stick anything on me'.

8 August — The Great Train Robbery. A gang robs the Glasgow–Euston mail train at Sears Crossing near Linslade, Bucks, escaping with £2,631,384.

October — Roy leaves for Paris with Tommy Gallagher, spending three months in France midget wrestling.

6 December — Roy Smith's daughter Karen Louise Smith born in a private maternity home in Hove. Roy flies back from Paris to see the baby and be with her mother, before returning to France where he and Tommy Gallagher continue their tour with appearances in Belgium, Switzerland and Portugal.

1964

26 March — The Great Train Robbery trial ends with the principals each receiving thirty-year prison sentences.

12 July — *Sunday Mirror* story suggesting a homosexual link between a famous peer and a leading London gangster; later admitted that the peer was Lord Boothby and the gangster, Ronnie Kray. Within three weeks the *Sunday Mirror* apologised and paid £40,000 damages to Booth-

by. Ronnie also received an apology – but no damages.

Roy Smith takes responsibility for his daughter Karen, taking her first to stay with his sister Elsie in Hillingdon; then to his brother Harry in South Benfleet, before the Krays find a family who will look after her in the East End.

16 December The Hideaway Club opened in Gerrard Street, Soho, by Huw Cargill McCowan, son of a Scottish baronet.

December Roy Smith opens in pantomime in Edmonton with Hughie Green.

21 December A Kray henchman arrives at the Hideaway Club to demand protection money. Reported later that their demand was for 20 per cent of the takings, rising to 50 per cent. In return they would provide two doormen, attract business to the club and keep away 'undesirable people'. When these demands are refused, the man proceeds to smash glasses, and damage the furniture and fittings.

1965

6 January Reggie and Ronnie Kray, described as company directors of the Glenrae Hotel, Seven Sisters Road, arrested and later remanded in custody accused of demanding money with menaces. Ronnie reported to have said: 'It's taken you long enough. This is all down to the *Mirror*. It was the same with Spotty.' Reggie said: 'All right. It's one of those things. You've got your job to do.'

Roy Smith joins them in Brixton Prison, also on remand, accused of deception and fraudulent conversion in a case involving a motor car belonging to Hughie Green and the sum of

£750, and another charge of deception concerning another person and the sum of £1,500.

12 February — The Lord Chancellor (Lord Gardiner) refuses the Krays' application for bail after hearing their application in camera. They are represented by Petre Crowder QC MP and Richard Du Cann QC. After a 1½-hour hearing the Lord Chancellor decides that he has no jurisdiction in the matter.

March — A juror is asked to stand down in the Kray trial after being heard to express an opinion about the outcome of the case.

5 April — The Kray trial collapses. After fifty-six days in custody, they are released immediately amid widespread allegations of jury-nobbling – and walk down the steps of the Old Bailey arm in arm. Later that day they announce that they have bought the Hideaway Club, and hold a celebration party there that evening. They later change its name to the El Morocco.

19 April — Reggie Kray marries Frances Shea at St James's Church, Bethnal Green. Guests include the boxers Terry Spinks and Ted 'Kid' Lewis. The wedding photos are taken by David Bailey. The honeymoon is spent in Athens.

25 April — A cautiously written story in *The Sunday People* links the Krays to Leslie Payne and Frederick Albert Gore, two of their associates, who had been involved in twenty-two companies that had all gone bankrupt.

Roy Smith spends sixteen weeks in summer season at Bournemouth, appearing in the water show *Gulliver's Travels*, followed by two weeks in Great Yarmouth with Rolf Harris. Reggie and Ronnie Kray travel down to see him in both shows, taking their mother and staying overnight.

	Estimated by Pearson that by now the Krays have international links with the Mafia. Amsterdam was then the centre for the stolen jewellery trade; Zurich for the arms dealers; Paris and the south of France for arts thefts; London and Geneva for gold. By then the Krays were also involved in drug distribution, the West End protection racket, fruit machines, and also the import and export of pornography. They had also been involved in handling stolen Canadian share certificates.
17 October	Full-page feature in *The Sunday People*, 'Fate's Final Blow at the Midget', details the birth of Karen, the failure of Roy Smith's marriage, and how he is now bringing up his daughter on his own.
21 December	Roy Smith opens in pantomime at the London Palladium, again playing Bonzo the dog in *Babes in the Wood*, with leading roles being taken by Frank Ifield, Arthur Askey, Sid James and Kenneth O'Connor. *The Stage* says this is 'the funniest panto in years'. The Krays see the show several times, afterwards being taken backstage by Smith to meet other artistes.
December	The Krays and their South London rivals the Richardsons meet at the Astor Club off Berkeley Square to discuss co-operation between the two 'firms' in their dealings with the Mafia. Both sides arrive heavily armed, but there is no violence, although the meeting ends with disagreement and acrimony.

1966

February	Roy Smith charged with causing actual bodily harm, after stabbing a man. He is released on bail, but eventually gaoled.
8 March	Richard Hart, a member of the Kray 'firm', is killed in a shoot-out at Mr Smith's Club in

	Catford, involving the Richardsons. The arrests that follow this fracas lead to the imprisonment of the Richardsons.
9 March	Ronnie Kray murders George Cornell in the Blind Beggar public house, shooting him in the head with a 9mm Mauser. Smith is with Ronnie that evening, but not at the Blind Beggar.
12 December	Frank Mitchell, 'The Mad Axe Man', is sprung from Dartmoor Prison by the Krays, who find him accommodation in Barking where Roy Smith visits him. On Christmas Eve, Mitchell leaves that address – and is never seen again. Roy Smith is one of the last to see him alive.
1967	
7 June	Frances Kray (23), wife of Reggie, commits suicide, taking a massive overdose of phenobarbitone. Coroner records a verdict of suicide while the balance of her mind was disturbed.
	On being released from Wandsworth Prison, Roy Smith returns to Soho and a 'Welcome Home' party at the El Morocco, organised by Reggie and Ronnie Kray.
	The Krays begin a major operation distributing purple hearts from an address in Soho, and also take over parts of the Richardsons' fruit machine operation. That summer two members of the firm, Jack Frost and Teddy Smith, disappear.
September	Roy Smith films an appearance in The Beatles' film *Magical Mystery Tour*, down at Shepton Mallet.
28–29 October	Reggie Kray murders Jack 'The Hat' McVitie.
6 November	Roy Smith marries Sylvia Alexander at Philpot Street register office, Stepney Green, and that

evening there is a party at the Alexander home, where his daughter Karen is being brought up by Sylvia's mother.

13 November — Roy Smith phones his wife from Heathrow Airport to say that he is 'disappearing for a little while'. He flies to Zurich, Cairo and Bangkok, going on to Japan before acquiring the necessary papers to work as a midget wrestler in Java, the Philippines and South Korea. He is away from home for nearly a year.

1968

February–March — The busker Don Partridge, who had worked with Roy Smith as a busker in Soho, has a hit single with the recording *Rosie*.

2 April — Ronnie Kray flies to Paris and then to New York, hoping to reach agreement with the American Mafia regarding gambling club operations in London.

9 May — Ronnie and Reggie Kray arrested in a Scotland Yard dawn swoop in which twenty-four London addresses are raided simultaneously by the police, and most known members of their 'firm' arrested.

6 July — Preliminary hearing of the case against the Krays held before the Chief Metropolitan Magistrate, Frank Milton.

2 November — Roy Smith arrives back from the Far East, and returns to the Alexanders' home in Stayner's Road, Stepney Green.

4 November — Roy Smith arrested at gun-point in a dawn raid. 'You're the midget,' said the police officers who were gathering evidence for the Kray case. Smith is released after seventy-two hours; they had insufficient evidence against him – and he says nothing!

1969

29 January	Roy Smith appears in the Buskers' Show at the Royal Albert Hall, with Don Partridge topping the bill. The show is filmed and subsequently shown around the world.
8 March	Ronnie and Reggie Kray, then aged 35, both sentenced to not less than thirty years' imprisonment for the Cornell and McVitie murders after a sensational trial at the Old Bailey presided over by Mr Justice Melford Stevenson.

1970

	Roy Smith opens a disco in Rhondda Grove, and also sets up a mini-cab business, Viceroy Minicabs, in Aberavon Road, Mile End, with eleven drivers. This business lasts for eighteen months. During this period he also runs two East End pubs.
13 October	Roy's son, Simon Martin Smith, born at Mile End Hospital.
November	Roy and his father-in-law take the baby Simon to live on a kibbutz in Israel for six weeks so that the baby can be baptised and circumcised in Israel. The baby's mother, Sylvia, remains in London.

1971

Summer	Roy Smith appears in a summer season show in Blackpool, where he has a dispute with Charlie Cairoli.
23 August	Roy Smith aborts a robbery at the Blackpool Tower when he finds the area suddenly swarming with police after the shooting of Supt Gerald Richardson.

1972

	Roy Smith sent to prison for seven years for the manslaughter of Frankie Randall, who dies

after being shot; Smith insists that although he did shoot at Randall, his shot missed – and that someone else fired the fatal shot. In Wandsworth Prison he becomes a close friend of the robber 'Chopper' Knight.

1975

8 January — Charlie Kray leaves Maidstone Prison after completing his ten-year sentence for his part in the Krays' affairs; he was sentenced to ten years for being an accessory to the murder of Jack McVitie, which he denied (and still denies), and was released after earning full remission. That evening their mother Violet holds a 'Welcome Home' party at the Blue Coat pub, Bishopsgate. Roy Smith is among the guests.

1976

December — Roy Smith found Not Guilty of deception after being accused of stealing twenty-two lambs, and also of causing actual bodily harm.

1977

February — Roy Smith gaoled again for twelve months, after his mother-in-law had taken a stolen ring to be valued by the same jeweller from whom he had stolen it.

29 September — The Blackwall Tunnel raid. An armed gang ambush a security van, stealing £95,000 in wage packets, having blocked the tunnel once the van was inside. Two shots are fired. A security guard is injured with a blow to the head.

1978

August — The Banstead security van raid. An armed gang attacks the van, using a chainsaw, and escapes with £780,000.

1979

November	Charles 'Chopper' Knight (39) sentenced to twenty-one years in gaol for the Blackwall Tunnel raid. He is said to have led a gang that had netted £1,750,000 from robberies. Judge Stocker says: 'I have no doubt that you were the leader – and a highly skilled one. Your qualities would have fitted you to be a leader in almost any field you might have chosen.' Knight was also sentenced to eighteen years for the Banstead raid and fifteen years for a raid on Rochester post office in which £79,000 was stolen. He was said to have been shopped by a supergrass just as he was planning to steal £3,500,000 in foreign currency that was due to be loaded on the *QE2* at Southampton. The supergrass gave details of fifty robberies in which Knight had been involved and named many of his accomplices.

1980

January	Roy Smith is back in Pentonville on remand for four months, again charged with deception. There he meets the rock star Hugh Cornwell, lead singer and guitarist with The Stranglers, who has been gaoled for two months on drug charges, and the Palladium bandleader Jack Parnell, who has also been sent to prison for drink–driving offences.

1982

5 August	Violet Kray dies.

1983

26 November	The Brink's Mat gold bullion robbery at Heathrow, in which £26m of gold is stolen in the biggest robbery in British history. Several of those concerned had been associated with the Krays in the sixties, and were well known in the Soho clubs.

1984

By now working as a busker in Leicester Square again, Roy Smith sleeps on the London Embankment for ten months until his fellow buskers learn of his plight and book him into the St Mungo hostel for homeless men in Endell Street, Covent Garden, in the September. He stays there until the New Year when he is thrown out after assaulting a fellow resident.

1986

11 January — Roy Smith returns to the St Mungo hostel in Covent Garden after a year spent staying with his daughter and kipping down with friends in various parts of London. This time he is given his own room, and settles.